Unleash your **Purpose** and **Productivity**
to **Get More** out of **Work** and **Life**.

YOUR WHY

How Some
ACHIEVE MORE
and Others Don't

MATTERS NOW

JUSTIN JONES-FOSU, SR

Published in Charlotte, North Carolina, by Peter Jones Publishing

Editor: Darcie Clemen
Cover Design: Sherwin Soy, orangepubkit.com
Interior Design: Katherine Lloyd, www.thedeskonline.com
Back Cover Author Picture: Bentley Crawford
Chapter Cartoons: Ricky Castillo
Venn Diagram: David Simion

The stories shared in this book are accurate to the best of the publisher's ability. Permission was obtained for each of the personal stories shared. A few of the names have been changed to protect their privacy. Any Internet addresses, phone numbers, or company or product information printed in this book are offered as a resource and are not intended in any way to be or to imply an endorsement by the publisher, nor does the publisher vouch for the existence, content, or services of these sites, phone numbers, companies, or products beyond the publication date of this book.

ISBN hardcover: 978-1-7365070-0-1
ISBN paperback: 978-0-9833718-4-7
ISBN ebook: 978-0-9833718-6-1

Printed in the United States of America

To my number two, who has all six of my names:
Peter, I love you, and you are a constant reminder of
why I work and why I want to come back home so quickly.
I even look forward to you asking the number-one
question of children everywhere—why!

Thank you to #teamjonesfosu for allowing me to
share my gift with the world and at your bedtime!

Contents

Chapter 1

MERGE:
It Takes Two
to Achieve More

As a professional I have often bounced back and forth between books focused on purpose (the Why of doing things) and books focused on passion (the Now of doing things). I have bounced back and forth between books focused on meaning (Why) and books focused on effort (Now). When I read books on purpose, I became more reflective, intentional, and mindful. I would then read books on passion and I would do, act, and accomplish more than before. But I often felt unsettled, as it seemed that I was giving up one for the sake of the other.

Have you felt that way? As if you are jumping back and forth, gaining in one area and losing in the other?

A person who is high Why (purpose/motivation) oriented

with little to no Now thinks a lot and plans a lot but can fail to act. A person who is high Now (passion/intensity) oriented with little to no Why makes bad decisions, rushes to judgment, and may confuse activity with progress. In which area do you tend to fall? Neither one of these extremes is healthy, and yet we need both the Why and the Now.

As the great philosophers Rob Base and DJ E-Z Rock once said, "It takes two to make a thing go right. It takes two to make it outta sight." As I struggled with my Why and my Now, I finally came to a great philosophical discovery of my own:

Why and Now are not mutually exclusive and can be merged together.

Wow! What a concept! Instead of swinging back and forth between the two extremes, you can put your Why and your Now together. You can merge purpose and passion, motivation and intensity. Further, if you can focus on the zone where these two areas overlap, you can *achieve more*.

And who among us doesn't want to achieve more?

When I began researching this and practicing merging my own Why and Now together, I tapped into a sweet spot of greater impact. I had to begin sharing this concept with my consulting clients. Over the last couple of years, the "Your Why Matters Now" concept has been my most popular presentation, and I consistently have conference participants and the organizations that hire me asking for more.

To be clear, Why and Now are not new concepts. Purpose (motivation, intent, reasons) and passion (intensity, productivity, effort) are ideas that have been talked about, researched, and written about for decades upon decades. There are people who have more degrees, more experience, and more gray hairs (they can have that one) who have studied these concepts inside and out. So why write another book about these ideas? Because I want to share this unique insight and perspective on merging the Why and the Now. I want to show you the practical approach that has inspired countless participants in my presentations and consulting to achieve more in their professional and personal lives.

BETTER TOGETHER

Think about two things that are good on their own but amazing together. What are you thinking about? I'm thinking about something many of us use every day—computers. Steve Jobs revolutionized computers in a very simple but profound way. He took the ancient form of calligraphy and combined it with the well-used form of typewriting, and he gave us the first real choice of computer fonts. In an address to Stanford students, Jobs said:

> Reed College at that time offered perhaps the best calligraphy instruction in the country. Throughout the campus every poster, every label on every drawer, was beautifully hand calligraphed. Because I had dropped out and didn't have to take the normal classes, I decided to take a calligraphy class to learn how to do this. I learned about serif and sans serif typefaces, about varying the amount of space between different letter combinations, about what makes great typography great. It was beautiful, historical, artistically subtle in a way that science can't capture, and I found it fascinating.
>
> None of this had even a hope of any practical application in my life. But ten years later, when we were designing the first Macintosh computer, it all came back to me. And we designed it all into the Mac. It was the first computer with beautiful typography. If I had never dropped in on that single course in college, the Mac would have never had multiple typefaces or proportionally spaced fonts. And since Windows just copied the Mac, it's likely that no personal computer would have them.[1]

These were two well-established things that when brought together were more impactful. There is also the robot that was combined with a vacuum to create a vacuum that smartly cleans floors and carpets while you go about your life doing other things. But let's get to the really serious merging. A peanut butter sandwich is good, and a jelly sandwich is good, but a peanut butter and jelly sandwich is exceptional. If that last example doesn't prove my thesis, nothing will.

Both your Why and your Now are needed to move from achieving to achieving more.

Both your Why and your Now are needed to move from achieving to achieving more. You need to tap into your purpose *and* activate your passion. But let me clarify: this type of achievement is not about comparing yourself to others but rather to yourself. When you activate the Achieve More Zone (AMZ), where the Why and Now intersect, you will begin moving toward your full potential in both your personal and your professional life.

As a consultant I have noticed a multitude of initiatives and books focused on how organizations can create a winning and engaging culture. As a bookstore lover and online book shopper, I have noticed a plethora of self-help, motivational, and professional development books tailored mainly to individuals inspiring themselves. We need both. I believe the partnership between organizational leadership/culture and the individual is important and should be fifty-fifty. In this book I will focus on the 50 percent belonging to you, the individual, as this is what you can directly control. I want to help you develop a sense of work ownership and achievement whether you work for yourself, for a company, or for your amazing, high-energy little kids.

If you are in a leadership role or aspiring to leadership, you'll get an extra benefit if you continue reading to the addenda. That's where I give some helpful thoughts and tips for how leaders can help their employees and team members embrace both their Why and their Now so that they don't merely achieve, but achieve more. Don't peek, though, because you do not want to miss what's coming first.

Your Why and Now will help you develop a sense of work ownership and achievement.

As you read and engage this book, be honest and vulnerable about where you really are and where you truly want to go. I also want you to think deeply, laugh (you know: that ugly, loud kind of laugh), and apply the tips where you see fit. Share these strategies and ideas with those you think can benefit. This will help you in your achievement journey; sharing your new knowledge will help you grasp the information and the tools on a deeper level.

By the end of this book, you will have a clearer understanding of your Why and your Now and how you can merge them to achieve more. You will know how to apply your Why at work, how to be more productive, and how to increase your effort. Each section contains tools to help you practically apply what you are learning. So buckle in and enjoy this brief but fun ride as we dive deeper into the Why, the Now, and what you can practically do to integrate both into your everyday life.

Part One

WHY:
Your Purpose and Motivation

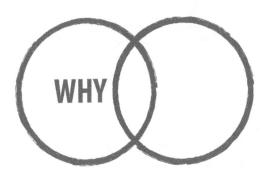

He who has a why to live can bear almost any how.

—Friedrich Nietzsche

Chapter 2

BEGIN:
Start with the Why in Mind

Phiona the Chess Queen

Phiona Mutesi grew up in the Katwe slums in Kampala, Uganda. As a young girl, she would wake up at five each morning to walk two hours to find a semblance of drinkable water. Her father died of AIDS when she was three years old, and a few weeks later her older sister died at a very young age. Phiona dropped out of school before she was nine.

There was a horrid stench and suffocating heat the day she followed her brother, Brian, to a rickety and ruined building where she discovered the game of chess. This was the same game that you and I know but under much rougher conditions. The chess board, if you want to call it that, was discolored and barely discernible. The chess pieces were severely damaged and dirty. But Phiona would receive a free cup of porridge by taking chess lessons, so she began walking nearly four miles every day to play chess.

Phiona eventually fell in love with the game, and that love led to her winning the Uganda junior girls' chess championship when she was eleven. That love led to her being one of three to represent Uganda at Africa's International Children's Chess Tournament, where she won! That love led her to compete internationally.

Phiona loved chess, but her real dream was to build a house outside of Katwe so her mom would never have to move again. Over the course of four years, Phiona's family had moved six times because of crumbling conditions and intimidating theft. This dream is what kept her going through all the hardship, failure, humiliation, and tireless nights—it was her Why!

Phiona's Why pushed her to walk nearly four miles and persist in a game that was widely considered exclusive to the educated and elite. Her Why led her to build the house for her mom, win several championships, and now she works to help inspire girls around the world. She has her own chess club and inspires Ugandan youth who suffer with poverty and a lack of hope. Phiona's purpose continues to motivate her to achieve more both for herself and for others.

Justin the Troubled Worker

In only my second job shortly after college, I worked for a Fortune 600 company (only 100 rankings off from the big dogs), and I started well. Before this new role, I had led a team of fifty people at a Fortune 50 company. I was excited to try something different and new and venture into a passion area of mine: training and development.

At first I was so excited about the opportunity. Then, little by little, events occurred that caused me to slowly fall out of love with it. The manager I initially worked for and loved left the company. Corporate politics started to suffocate my spark and innovation, and I desperately dreaded coming to work. At first, I blamed everyone else. I blamed my new manager, I blamed the culture of corporate politics (I still blame this one), and I blamed myself for deciding to work for this company. Things got bad. I was given the black mark of working professionals everywhere—I was put on a "performance improvement plan" (gasp). This was a big deal. At the time, I was newly married, thinking about kids, and beginning to wonder if I would even have a job to support my family.

I talked to mentors; I talked to friends—heck, I even talked to my friend the mirror a lot! I began to take ownership, and things improved slowly but surely. It even reached the point where they wanted to promote me.

What caused this turnaround? What kept me going through all the internal and external challenges? What allowed me to persevere and even eventually thrive? My Why! My Why was to eventually create a business that would inspire others to take positive action and challenge what they believed was possible. This led me to continue growing professionally and learning from even the most challenging experiences at that job and beyond.

What about you? What has been your story? What has been your purpose? What has kept you going, led you to persevere and not give up? While you may not play chess and have a Disney movie (*Queen of Katwe*) made after you, and while you may never get put on a performance improvement plan, what will keep you going as you encounter new challenges, new issues, and new headaches? Your Why!

WHY YOUR WHY IS IMPORTANT

Why is your Why important anyway? There has been a lot of conversation about Why over the past few years. With Simon Sinek's amazing best-selling book *Start with Why*, many people were inspired to understand their Why as leaders, organizations, and as individuals. What is this Why that everyone is talking about? If I could give it a synonym, I would call it *purpose*. It is important because it is the thing that motivates and drives us. It can also be called our intentions or the fuel that keeps us going. Understanding and living by our Why has been shown to help us work better, engage better, and ultimately live better. The Why has been shown to help people develop and build resilience, find meaning at work, and focus on the things that matter.

An attitude of resilience increases our effort and our chances of achievement.

Think about it this way. Imagine you are getting ready to leave work and there are several people around. You ask for something to drink. What drink are you asking for? Many people might offer you suggestions as to the best drink for them or what they think you need. The gym addict may offer you a protein shake, the happy-hour enthusiast may offer you a glass of red wine, the dieter may offer you some good old-fashioned lemon water, the Willy Wonka fan may offer you something supersweet, and the "I can't get out of bed in the morning" professional may offer you some black coffee (shaken, not stirred). Which is the right drink?

You are right! It depends on *why* you are asking for a drink. Are you asking to be healthy, to be energized, to focus, or to stay hydrated? Are you asking because you want to relax, to rinse out your mouth, or because you had a long day at work? What if you don't understand why you want a drink in the first place? You will probably take the first suggestion that sounds good to you. Unfortunately, this is normal, as we have been conditioned to simply do and not always ask why. Understanding why you're asking for a drink impacts what you should drink. I have noticed too many people symbolically drinking things that don't match up to their Why. When I look at my past, I see myself drinking things that did not match my Why. What about you? What have you been drinking, and does it align with your Why? If it does align, there is always room for growth. If it doesn't align, let's change that as we move forward together.

Your Why gives you a competitive advantage, because if you are operating from your Why, you are usually working with great passion and focus. When you understand why you are doing something, it motivates you to give your all. People intrinsically connect more with why they do rather than simply what they do.

People intrinsically connect more with why they do rather than simply what they do.

Our Why is also vital for helping us remember why we started something in the first place. I have noticed that we usually start something and get super excited, and then after a while we forget why we began in the first place. Think about it. Have you ever purchased a new car and loved it? You couldn't stop smelling it and hugging it, and then six to nine months later, you were looking for a new car. What about a new apartment or home? Do you remember that first day you walked in and almost cried? A year or so later, you are fed up with the lousy place. What about that new job, or position, or title? How excited you were to get into that industry and have a fresh start—all to be disappointed and run down by the day-to-day happenings. Let's make it personal. What about your personal relationships (marriage, friendships, roommates, relatives)? Do you remember when you first said, "I do," and nowadays you sometimes wonder if you should have said, "I don't"? I have seen this happen in myself and others too many times. Reconnecting to our Why is important for us to remember our original intentions and to challenge our cultural pattern of always wanting the next thing. We cannot lose sight of the value of our current state and where we have been. (This is the friction between contentment and complacency, which we will cover in part 2.) Our Why helps us remember the value of things that have been in our lives, even those things that have been there a very long time.

THE GREAT PHILOSOPHERS

The great philosophers of our time have shared the importance of the Why. You know who those great philosophers are, right?

Children! What is the number-one question children ask? You guessed it: why, why, why, why, why. I probably could have added a couple more too. This is a natural question that we asked a lot when we were children. As we have gotten older, we've replaced that *why* with *what*, *how*, and *when*. It's as if we have forgotten the golden question that helps us understand the world. The question that helps us develop intentions and motivations about what we do and how we do it.

I used to be that kid who asked why all the time to my mother. Many of my peers' parents, grandparents, or guardians would simply reply with a stern, "Because I said so." That response has conditioned many children, who become teens, who become adults, who become professionals, to stop asking why. But that question has never left; it just lies dormant inside us. I am grateful that my mom chose to tell me why she would ask me to do things—why I had to wash the dishes and why I had to stop picking my nose (thanks, Mom).

Let me give you a prime example. I remember when I was a paperboy (my second entrepreneurial pursuit) and made some pretty good money for a thirteen-year-old. I came home once with a New York Knicks Starter jacket, and my mom asked me about the jacket and how much it cost. I told her seventy-five dollars, and she immediately made me take it back. I was M-A-D! I had used my own money from the job where I worked my butt off, and she was making me take it back. At the time, I vehemently agreed with Will Smith that "parents just don't understand." But Mom later told me why. She didn't want me to spend that kind of money on a coat when I could get a similar-quality coat for less. While I hated her for it then, I love her for it now, as I am not enamored with having the latest fashions and trends (except my amazing smartphone). When I do shop for clothes, I look on the clearance racks, and I may find name brands there. This is something that in the long run has made me better, but it took embracing the number-one kid question.

We desperately want to be those kid philosophers at work *and* in our personal lives. We want to ask the following why questions over and over again!

1. Why are there so many meetings (and meetings about meetings)?
2. Why do I receive so many emails?
3. Why do people hate each other so much?
4. Why can't people respect each other even if they disagree?
5. Why does one event happen and people see it so differently?
6. Why don't people just give me money?
7. Why are there so many meetings (did I say this one already)?

It's time we turn back into those little kids and begin asking why again.

THE FOUNDATION PYRAMID

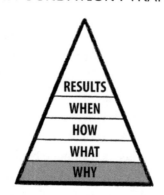

Our Why has great implications for our work. It impacts our focus, our drive, and our productivity. Imagine that there are three workers working on granite and each is asked what he is doing. The first says, "I am not sure, but I am being paid to do it." The second worker says, "I am making granite for some structure." The third worker proudly says, "I really love what I am doing. I am making a historical monument for one of the greatest civil rights leaders in America: Dr. Martin Luther King Jr." Which worker do you think is going to produce the best results? The one who knows the Why! While both are needed, why we do is vastly more important than simply knowing what we do. When we know why we are doing something, it really does impact what we do, how we do it, and when we do it, which can lead to amazing results.

In any individual task, project, or assignment, these five aspects—why, what, how, when, and the results—can be thought of as a pyramid with the Why as the foundation. (You could also add who if you are looking through an organizational lens.)

I am one of the biggest Stephen Covey fans you will meet. I read his *The 7 Habits of Highly Effective People* when I was in my early teens. (I even carried a Franklin Planner to school. Thanks, Mom.) I still practice the habit of beginning with the end in mind. While I definitely do not disagree with this habit, I believe the spirit of Covey's writing would include beginning with the Why in mind. Do you see why? You could start with what you envision at the end, but if you do not know your Why, you may end up in the wrong place. While we begin with the end in mind, we should also think about how our Why feeds into that end we truly desire.

When you don't know your Why, you may find yourself in the wrong place.

The Foundation Pyramid helps us see the layers we encounter. *Why* we do something (purpose and motivation) impacts *what* we do (our task), which impacts *how* we do it (technique and effort), which leads to *when* we do it (timing), which ultimately impacts our *results* (outcome). Some people start with *what*, but doing that means a smaller foundation. Without the Why to build on, the results will be less powerful. Including the Why means a larger, more stable foundation on which to build the great and meaningful results that all of us want to enjoy. When the Why is the foundation, people achieve more in the long term not because they have to, but because they get to.

MOTIVATION MATTERS

One way to think about our Why is as motivation. Motivation has many definitions. One of those definitions is a psychological process that gives an individual's behavior a sense of purpose and direction. An internal drive to satisfy an unsatisfied need. It has also been defined as "a series of energizing forces that originate both with and beyond an individual's self. These energizing forces determine behavior and impact productivity."[1] Motivation can be intrinsic and extrinsic, which we will discuss further in chapter 3.

People who are motivated generate more effort toward their work than those who are not motivated. Those who are motivated are also impacted by their motives, which leads to behavioral change. When a person is motivated, he or she directs intentional effort toward specific actions to perform in such a way to achieve the intended goal. Organizations are asking for and sometimes demanding more motivation from their employees and members, but organizations must be willing to change how they motivate. In his best-selling book *Drive*, Daniel Pink describes modern motivation, or what he calls "Motivation 3.0," as a move away from fulfilling basic needs, receiving rewards, and being threatened with punishment, and a move toward learning, creating, improving the world, and ultimately doing work that matters.[2]

People who are motivated generate more effort toward their work than those who are not motivated.

It's important to note the three levels of motivation. There is amotivation (not motivated), extrinsic motivation (motivated by external things, e.g., money, rewards), and intrinsic motivation (motivated by internal things, such as the love of the work itself). Research has shown repeatedly that while extrinsic motivation has the power to move people forward in the short term, people are able to achieve more with intrinsic motivation. The next chapter will help you tap into that intrinsic motivation—your Why.

KEY TAKEAWAYS AND TIPS

p When you start with the Why in mind, it fuels what you do, how you do it, and when you do it, and ultimately it can lead to amazing results.

p Your Why is important because it serves as a motivator, a guide, and as your competitive advantage at work.

p To live a life of purpose and meaning, we need to tap into that inner child and keep asking why.

Chapter 3

CHOOSE:
Not All Whys
Are Created Equal

Lydia M.: Wife and Litigation Attorney

The distraught teacher forcefully slammed the seventh-grade classroom door and yelled at everyone to sit down immediately. He was extremely angry, and this anger was directed at the defiant Lydia. Lydia had just yelled at him, and he was no longer going to take it. He narrowed his eyes at Lydia and pointedly asked her, "Do you want to be like your sisters?" Immediately, Lydia started to cry. It was a reality check. Lydia thought to herself, "If I keep getting kicked out of class and written up, I'll never live up to my full potential."

Lydia grew up rough, in a single-parent household in southeastern Virginia. Outside her home were drugs, violence, and gangs. Inside her home she had two sisters. One had had her first child by age fifteen and continued to have another child almost every year until she reached her fifth child. The other sister was in a group home for troubled teens. Lydia's sisters were so rebellious that they had been kicked out of class, suspended from school, and even sent to juvenile detention before they both dropped out of school altogether. Her seventh-grade teacher knew her sisters, and when he asked if she wanted to be like her sisters, this was not a compliment. Lydia pondered her teacher's question, and as the tears rolled down her face, she knew she had to be motivated more than what she saw in and around her home.

That day in class was a turning point. Lydia committed herself to being different. With lots of hard work, she ended up graduating from college, graduating law school, and is now practicing law in a major US city. Lydia shares how her motivation has driven her when she says, "I'm not really living my life for myself. I live my life first for God. Second for my future children. I don't want them to struggle and go through the things that I went through, or see the things that I've seen, or feel the way that I've felt. Third, for my ancestors. To honor them, I want to live the best life that I can live." Lydia's Why propelled her to greatly achieve.

As I have spent nearly a decade studying the concept of discovering one's Why/purpose, I have found that a person's Why exists somewhere on a spectrum in three distinct areas. Where your Why falls in these areas can exponentially change the impact of your Why and the results you achieve. These areas are: type of Why (macro and micro), the motivation for your Why (intrinsic and extrinsic), and the level of your Why (high and low). Will you choose to be different and operate with an intrinsically motivating high Why?

MACRO VERSUS MICRO

As stated before, I am a huge fan of Simon Sinek's work *Start with Why*. His TED Talk on the golden circle has exponentially accelerated this conversation of purpose and how it impacts every-thing we do.[1] One of the things that Sinek has shared is that we only have one Why that impacts everything else we do, and for the most part I agree with that statement. What he calls the "one Why" I call the "Macro Why," but where I add to this work is that we also have Micro Whys. Let me explain.

My Macro Why is, "I inspire others to take purposeful action so that they achieve authentic results by challenging the bound-aries of what they believe is possible." This Macro Why should permeate everything I do, and for the most part, it does. My Macro Why is the lens through which I look at life; it impacts things such as my career choices, volunteering opportunities, and even my hobbies. The Macro Why is the big picture. It is the imprint on your life. You can think of it as the tree trunk of your life and the branches as the Micro Whys. With this big-picture perspec-tive, you can assess whether your life is moving in the intended direction.

Micro Whys are helpful in the bucket areas of our lives. Those are areas such as friends, health, finances, education, community service, family, and work. Now, while my Macro Why certainly unfolds into the Micro Whys, they are slightly different. Let me share an example. My Micro Why for exercising is to be healthy so that as my kids get older, I can still run around and play with them. I also need to be healthy to live out my achievement hobby of trek-king/mountain climbing. I remember watching *The Biggest Loser* and seeing the coaches ask the contestants, "Why are you here? What is motivating you to stay here and to get healthy?" Many times you would hear: "For my spouse [or kids]," or "So I can return to the shape of my 'playing days'!" There can certainly be overlap in our Macro and Micro Whys, but they aren't the exact same.

Your Micro Why, while different, should be influenced by your Macro Why.

When I am keynoting a conference or conducting a workshop for professionals, I may ask, "What was your Why for getting into your industry?" Some participants answer, "To make a difference." I also sometimes ask, "Why did you decide to work for your organization?" Some participants answer, "Because of the impact I can have within the organization." I also ask, "Why did you marry your spouse [or get into that relationship]?" Some participants answer, "I don't know." Ha! Most really answer because they saw something special in him or her and could see a future with that person. When I speak at educational institutions, I may ask, "Why is college important?" or "Why did you choose this school?" or "Why did you choose your major?" So again, we have one Why that I call our Macro Why, but we also have Micro Whys for specific areas of our lives. The Micro Why should support and align with your Macro Why. While the Micro Whys have a more specific focus, like the branches of a tree they should shoot out from the main trunk, the Macro Why.

INTRINSIC VERSUS EXTRINSIC

Our brains are wired for two types of motivation. We are either driven by intrinsic motivation (motivation that comes from inside ourselves, internal rewards, something we enjoy just for the fun of it, or because we believe it is the right thing to do) or extrinsic motivation (motivation that comes from external sources, external rewards, and driven by tangible pressures or rewards) to achieve a goal, result, or outcome. It can sometimes be challenging to embrace your intrinsic, value-based motivation. Thus, many people are dominated by external motivation. Trust me: I have done this often. I am not saying that we should abandon all societal challenges for our own "personal" good. For example, you may have an individual who has a family but doesn't like his job. In a struggling economy, it may be challenging for him to find a new one. He should not just quit because his job doesn't fit his personal agenda. On the other hand, a person should not be in a profession or choose a major just because that is what society loves at the moment. As you begin to find, uncover, and rediscover your Why (both Macro and Micro), I encourage you to let it flow from an intrinsic place.

Intrinsic motivation is when you are performing an activity for the activity itself and you are inherently interested. You receive pleasure, enjoyment, and satisfaction in the activity alone. It is a type of autonomous motivation where participation is its own reward. Individuals who are intrinsically motivated tend to focus on growth, mastery, personal achievement, and developing competency in an area. Some of the characteristics you find in those who are intrinsically motivated are acceptance of challenges, curiosity, control, and imagination. Some people associate intrinsically motivated work with something you would do if money weren't an issue, or put a different way, "What would you do for free?"

Extrinsic motivation is when you are performing an activity for the reward or outcome it can get you. It generally is motivated by external pressures, societal norms, and some type of tangible reward. When people are extrinsically motivated, they may focus on displaying their ability for others. They are motivated by things such as salary, fame, money, grades, a promotion, company car, and so on.

While there are certainly benefits for both, *Science* magazine confirms that intrinsic rewards are more associated with positive outcomes and long-term success. A study of West Point cadets found that "cadets with primarily internal motives were about 20 percent more likely to make it through West Point than the average." Even cadets with mixed motives were less successful at sticking with a military career and being promoted early.[2] Intrinsic motivation definitely seems to offer the ability to achieve more.

I remember growing up as a teenager and reading leadership books at night when I was supposed to be sleeping. I would walk down the street with a book in my hand and my Franklin Planner in the other (stop judging me). I loved learning about leading others and leading myself. It fascinated me. I didn't need a prompt or reminder, because I loved to do it. What is that love for you? I see it almost every night when I see my amazing kids lying in bed, dreaming about how they will positively impact the world and create a more sustainable future. I am inspired by seeing them get so excited about their businesses and practical ways they can inspire their generation of peers.

When you are intrinsically motivated, you persist at difficult tasks and perform better because you are focused on learning (getting better) and not merely performance (showing that you are good). Extrinsic motivation (aka if-then rewards) can hurt your drive for intrinsic motivation, limit creativity, encourage unethical shortcuts, and breed short-term thinking. When intrinsic motivation is activated, it drives you to act because you find it engaging, interesting, and challenging.

Intrinsic motivation moves you to learning, getting better, and growing.

Herzberg's two-factor theory helps us understand this. In this theory, extrinsic factors, such as salary, job security, and working conditions, can lead to dissatisfaction if not met but do not necessarily lead to work satisfaction if met. The intrinsic factors, such as work itself and achievement, are motivators and satisfying by themselves.

People who are more intrinsically motivated are more involved in their jobs, put forth greater effort, and achieve more goals.[3] To be very clear, depending on the context, extrinsic rewards are good drivers if basic needs aren't being met. However, they usually point to people being motivated by things like providing for one's family or living a certain quality of life.

There is a distinct difference in what motivates people, but also in how much people are motivated. Next we'll look at the third area where Whys can differ.

HIGH VERSUS LOW

A person can have a Why, but I have noticed people have different levels of Why, or as I like to say, they are connected to their Why differently. When a person has a High Why, they have what I call the three Cs. They have *Clarity* about their Why, *Connection* to their Why, and *Consistency* with their Why.

When you have a High Why, you are clear about your Macro and Micro Whys. You can probably recite them over and over again. You understand your purpose and intentions. Your Why drives and motivates you constantly. If you were at the gym on the treadmill and somebody jumped on the treadmill next to you and asked, "What is your Why?" you would be able to answer that question. (Word of advice: don't run around gyms asking people their Whys, as it can come off as a little creepy, and these people in uniforms and badges that read *Security* might approach you.) If I asked you what your Why is right now, would you be able to tell me? So, what is it? It's okay if you do not know, because in the next chapter you will begin or rejoin the discovery process. When you have a Low Why, you don't really know why you are here or why you are doing something. You might just kind of exist, and you wouldn't be able to answer that person on the treadmill next to you.

When you have a High Why, you are also very connected to your Why. It means something to you. When you think about it, it should make you laugh or smile. The thought of not fulfilling it should make you sad. When you talk to people about it, it should energize and excite you. You get goose bumps when you talk about it. Low Whys can be identified if you aren't strongly connected to your Why or if your why doesn't do anything to you. If you do not feel connected to your Why, it may be vague, the wrong Why, outdated, or something that is purely external that needs an internal connection. You should connect to your Why in a very internal and visceral way. You should feel it!

A High Why also has a high level of consistency. You keep

your Why before you in what I call your "Why symbols," which are things like pictures, quotes, objects, and even your actual Why statement (we'll talk more about Why symbols in chapter 13). These constantly remind you and challenge you to measure things according to your Why. You may have it up on the wall at home or stored in your phone. It is that important to you that you want to see it. When you have a Low Why, you don't really care about seeing it, and you may only occasionally remember it.

You should connect to your Why in a very internal and visceral way. You should feel it!

One thing that is also helpful for a High Why is the focus on other people. A Why that is only about you is a very shortsighted Why. People who have stronger Whys understand how their Why impacts and makes a difference in the lives of other people. This could include your family, your community, or society in general. In chapter 4 we will dive deeper into why this can help your Why, but know that a strong Why includes a focus on others and not just yourself.

If you read all that and are thinking, *I need to work on my Why*, then you are in the right place, because in the next chapter you are going to begin the process of discovering or uncovering your Why. It's in there, and it's time to get it out. Are you ready?

KEY TAKEAWAYS AND TIPS

p Your Macro Why is the big-picture Why (the tree trunk) that encompasses your intentions and purpose. Your Micro Whys (the branches) encompass the different specific motivations you might have for the "bucket" areas of your life (e.g., health, friends, education).

p Your Why will be most productive when it flows out of intrinsic motivations, not extrinsic motivations. While there are times that outside pressures and ideals are helpful, you should identify the best course of action based on your values and ideals.

p A person with a High Why will have Clarity of their Why, Connection to their Why, and Consistency with their Why.

p Stay connected to your Why by keeping it before you on a consistent basis. Whether it is a letter you read, a picture you constantly look at, or a symbol that has great meaning to you, review it on a regular basis to maintain your connection with it.

Chapter 4

DISCOVER: What Is Your True Why?

Josh Parker: Husband, Father, Instructional Coach, and 2012 Maryland Teacher of the Year

"You look funny," "Go back to church, church boy," and "You can't even play basketball, nerd" were some of the things that Josh heard growing up. While Josh was extremely intelligent and bright, he was also a victim of bullying and often dealt with the pain of not fitting in. It was difficult for him not to have someone who would stand up for him as an ally. With this void, his allies later became writings, poems, and authors like Langston Hughes. He funneled his pain into his books. This pain eventually led Josh to quit sports broadcasting to become a teacher and an advocate for children. Josh stated, "The pain of not being accepted and the pain of being rejected and feeling alone are some of the 'Why' catalysts for me, because I didn't want people to feel that way. I want people to feel connected to other people, whether that be in print or in person . . . I feel that the pain from not being able to solve some of my own problems when I was a child, it propelled me to understanding why solutions matter." He tapped into one of his major life experiences to discover his Why of being a problem solver, and that led to his being a first-class teacher and ally for all children. Josh discovered his Why from his childhood pain.

What is your Why? At this moment, if you're thinking, "What is the meaning of my life?" then you are onto something. In this chapter you will begin to uncover your Macro Why and develop tools to uncover your Micro Whys. Let's dive into the really good stuff! For this section you may want a piece of blank paper or a whiteboard to be able to follow along and actually write some things down. It's pretty simple and no math is needed . . . yet!

UNCOVERING YOUR MACRO WHY

Your Macro Why is already in you—it just takes a little digging to pull it out. It has been shaped by many things in your life, including faith, family, successes, and failures. Your experiences growing up and as an adult have aided in the development of your Macro Why. Once you know what it is, I find it helpful to create a simple, one- or two-sentence statement defining your Macro Why. I call this the Macro Why Statement, or MaWS for short.

Following is a series of questions that will help you as you develop your Macro Why Statement (MaWS). Set aside fifteen to thirty minutes to answer as many of them as possible. Please do not skip this! You may be tempted to just brush through this area, but I encourage you not to. This is foundational, and even if you think you already know your MaWS, this may help you further clarify it. Think of this time as personal excavation!

You may have more than one answer to each question. That's fine—write them all down! For example, these are my answers to question 11 from the 12 Uncovering Questions that follow.

Question 11: **What do you believe about the world? What do you think the world should be like?**

- *I believe that people should be authentic.*

- *I believe work can be amazing and meaningful.*

- *I believe that people can achieve more than they thought was possible.*

- *I believe learning doesn't have to be either engaging or filled with practical content. I believe it can be both.*

- *I believe people can disagree and still respect each other.*

- *I believe people should take action that is aligned to their values (I still struggle with this sometimes).*

Now it's your turn. Grab a pen and a notebook, get comfortable, and let's uncover your Macro Why:

The 12 Uncovering Questions

1. Why are you here?
2. What major life experiences have you faced, both positive and negative?
3. What interested you growing up?
4. What gets you out of bed in the morning?
5. What interests and intrigues you in life?
6. What do you wish was better in the world?
7. Have you ever had a moment when you felt like you came alive? What were you doing, and why did that make you feel amazing?
8. What impact do you have on others/society? What impact do you want to have on others/society?
9. When have you felt inspired, hopeful, full of learning and growing?
10. What excites you?

11. What do you believe about the world? What do you think the world should be like?
12. How are others better after time with you or by what you do?

If you just spent time answering those questions, well done! It can be so easy to skip things like this, but this exercise is important for your journey ahead.

If you want to dig even deeper, try pairing the 7 Layers Deep exercise with the 12 Uncovering Questions. This is where you answer a question and you keep asking, "Why?" or "Why is that important?" until you can't go any further or until you get to the seventh layer. Here's an example:

What excites me? *Climbing mountains.* Why? *Because I love reaching the peak* (first why). Why? *Because it helps me feel like I've accomplished something* (second why). Why is that important? *Because I love challenges* (third why). Why? *Because it helps me believe that I can accomplish things that are hard* (fourth why). Why is that important? *Because I have set self-limiting boundaries on what I think is possible in my life* (fifth why). Why? *Because growing up I was told I couldn't succeed at hard things based on my circumstances* (sixth why, end of exercise).

I excavated to the sixth level before I felt I couldn't go anymore, but what about you? What did you uncover? Some people start off real deep and others on the surface, but ask yourself *Why?* or *Why is this important?* until you can't go anymore.

How did it feel answering the questions? I know it was tough for me as I explored my childhood. Answering some of those questions even made me cry as I had to go to some tough places in my past and uncover some painful memories. If that was the case for you too, *thank you* for taking the time and courage to dig deep. You will be better for it.

Now, if you are currently processing some things that you feel are more than overwhelming, I implore you to reach out to a professional for advice. It's important. Some people may need a little break here, and that's understandable. Come back to this later or tomorrow if you need to. When you feel you can continue after this uncovering procedure, let's move forward.

Your Macro Why Statement

Now let's take those answers and use them to create your Macro Why Statement (MaWS). I use the "I_ in order to___" format. This method will help you take those experiences and create a powerful statement to guide what you do.

THE "I___IN ORDER TO____" FORMAT

As you look at the answers to your 12 Uncovering Questions, what common threads do you see? Did you find a focus of being outside the box, inspiring others, supporting others, challenging the status quo, or something else significant? How has your life story, both the good and the bad, shaped who you are? What key words do you consistently come across? To be clear, this exercise is not about *what you do*, but about *why you do it*. A really good MaWS should tell your technique or process. The MaWS is bigger than our career and work roles—it should focus on the big picture and the impact you have on others.

How has your life story, both the good and the bad, shaped who you are?

When you have some of those common threads, create your MaWS by filling in this statement: "I [your contribution], in order to [impact to others and society]." Focus on creating a statement that fits you and viscerally makes sense to you rather than creating the "perfect" statement.

Here is my MaWS statement the wrong way and the right way:

A Little Off: I inspire kids through mentoring in order to help them grow up to be healthy adults.

Do you see why this is wrong? I have included what I do, and my MaWS should be bigger than my what. Can this statement work when I am not mentoring kids? No.

A Little Off: I speak fifty to sixty-five times a year to professionals and students in order to inspire them to make a difference in their lives at work and home.

What's wrong with this one? Again, I am sharing the specifics of what I do, not the overarching theme of why I am doing it. My contribution is too specific. Let's try this one.

Right-On: I inspire others to take purposeful action in order to help them achieve authentic results by challenging the boundaries of what they believe is possible.

This is right-on because I am sharing the overarching theme of why I do what I do. I have taken the themes from my 12 Uncovering Questions of challenging boundaries, authenticity, action, and inspiration as cues to develop the sentence. This statement applies to all my work activities (speaking, writing, consulting) and focuses on what I provide to others, not simply on the benefits to me.

GET FEEDBACK AND MAKE IT YOUR OWN

If you're going through multiple drafts of your MaWS, don't worry—it took me a while to reword things, too, and I even asked my friends for feedback. I posted my statement on Facebook to see if those who have come in contact with me through my work and my life agreed. They did agree, with some minor tweaks. While your MaWS shouldn't be based on others' opinions, it is helpful to understand honest perceptions of those close to you.

I want to caution you not to imitate my statement, and the reason I say that is because I tried to imitate others. I initially had something like, "To help people see the best version of themselves." That sounds good, right? Unfortunately, I had heard that somewhere and thought it sounded cool, but when I tested it with some close friends, they said, "I have never heard you say that before, and it just doesn't fit." That process was helpful for me, so I would encourage you to do the same. Ask three to five of your closest family, friends, and colleagues to critique your MaWS. Ask them if they feel it fits you. Hear their perspective and really listen, but know that at the end of the day, this is your statement, and it should excite you.

When you read your statement over and over, it should feel like you are pumping energy and emotion into your life, because that's how jazzed you are about it! Don't worry if it's not perfect yet; you can continue to come back and refine it until you get it just right. Please do not overthink this process—try to go with what feels right. You are not being graded on this, so do not feel like it has to be earth-shattering. Also, use language that makes sense for you. Don't try to make it sound academic (if you are not academic) or supercool (if you don't use supercool language), and for the love of me, please do not make it out of GIFs or emoji!

How Your Work Intersects with Your Macro Why

At this point you may be wondering how your work intersects with your Macro Why. We will talk more about this in the coming chapters, but here are three options to consider: (1) Keep doing amazing work because your existing work aligns perfectly with your Macro Why, (2) Identify ways to align your Why with your work in your current role or maybe another aspirational role at your company or as an entrepreneur, or (3) Consider finding new work at the appropriate time that makes sense for you and your key personal stakeholders. Let me share some great questions you can ask about the work you do:

1. When have you felt your best at work and when have you felt your worst? (Why, what was happening, and who was involved? Be specific.)
2. Why did you choose to enter your profession or industry?

3. Why did you start working as an entrepreneur, at your place of employment, or at home?
4. What makes you consistently smile when you are at work?
5. Does what you do now fit with your Macro Why?

DEVELOPING YOUR MICRO WHYS

Now, you don't need a specific statement for every one of your Micro areas, but only where it makes sense for you. As stated before, your Micro areas are areas such as family, finances, friends, hobbies, volunteering, health, and so on.

What motivates you to be excellent in your family, or to wake up every morning and go work out? (I hear your groans all the way through this book.) Knowing why you are doing something in these specific areas will help you persevere when things become overwhelming. When you don't want to go work out, will you remind yourself of your Micro Why? When you are deciding on purchases and the budget, will you remind yourself of why you are trying to get out of debt or stay out of debt? When you are contemplating doing something out of line with your faith (or you already did it), will you remember why your faith is important to you? These statements can be framed in a way that makes sense for you. You can use the "I___ in order to___" format or change it slightly to "I will so that_." Or you can create your own method—just make sure you are clear on that life value and the impact it will have.

Knowing why you do things will help you persevere when things are overwhelming.

Let me share my family's unofficial financial Micro Why: *We will become debt-free and handle our money with wisdom, so that we will be able to give like no one else (shout-out to Dave Ramsey) and serve our church, the community, and complete strangers with much of what we have.* Seven years ago, we were more than $120,000 in debt, and we faced some major decisions on how we would live. We sold a car, lived on a budget, and made some big changes to how we were spending. Last November we paid off our last student loan and are now 100 percent debt-free. It was a long and arduous journey, but this Micro Why helped us pay off that $120,000 in seven years. It continues to help us as we make important financial decisions regarding schooling for our children. Without this clarity from our Micro Why, we may have made a few decisions we would later regret.

Your Micro Whys will help you to better understand the more specific areas of your life. With better clarity of both your Macro Why and your Micro Whys, you will have a better grasp on your motivations for where you are going. Your Macro Why will help guide your big-picture life, and your Micro Whys will continue to drive the specific areas of your life with great purpose! Knowing your Why is important for all areas of your life, including where you probably spend the most time in your day: work.

KEY TAKEAWAYS AND TIPS

p Your Macro Why is shaped by your experiences, desires, successes, and failures.

p Your Macro Why is the big-picture Why that guides your life, while your Micro Why is for specific areas of your life (e.g., health, hobbies, family, etc.).

p Your Macro Why Statement should be in the format of "I ___ so that___" and it should include your impact on other people.

p When working on either your Macro Why Statement or your Micro Whys, do not get tripped up by trying to make them perfect. You want to be inspired by your statement, not stuck by it.

Chapter 5

ENRICH:
Your Why at Work

Jake Kahut: Sales Representative and Former Division 1 Football Player/Coach

Sitting at his desk, Jake hangs up the phone. He has been told no close to a hundred times today as he calls on existing and potential clients. Yesterday was different. Yesterday several people said yes, and Jake made a sale. No matter what, Jake reminds himself to stay positive, because after all, being negative will not help him. Jake is a different type of sales representative. He is the best kind. He is never rude and really enjoys helping his clients. Even if he is told no by a prospective client, he still makes it his mission to bring a smile to that person's face. Jake says, "You have to stay positive, because you're being told no one hundred times a day, and that one yes is what's really going to help with that. Because you know you can help them."

While other sales reps may get down on those challenging days, Jake crafts a way to stay engaged. He says, "Seriously, it's really rewarding when you know that you're helping someone. You just have to know some days you're going to get zero. Some days you're going to get ten, but you must stay the course." He also builds camaraderie, a similar camaraderie to what he had when he played and coached Division 1 football. He and the guy next to him high-five when they make a sale. They also play a game to keep the prospect on the phone, because the longer they can keep a prospect on the phone, the better the chances of making a sale. While Jake and his fellow sales rep are never rude, this is one of the ways they make it fun.

By bringing a smile to everyone's face and building camaraderie (Jake's Micro Why), Jake makes his seemingly unsexy job sexy to him! He crafts a meaningful experience in his job by tapping into his Micro Why. He is an example of a person who is able to add meaning and cross his Why bridges at work (more on that in a minute), and both he and his job are better because of it.

This chapter will lead you to developing your Why at work. When dealing with Whys at work, it is important to identify how to develop meaningful work, craft your job role, and move from seeing your work only as a job to seeing it as a career or calling. Like Jake, you can make your work meaningful.

MAKING WORK MEANINGFUL

Most adults spend an enormous amount of time at work, and for many, work is a great place of belonging. A survey conducted by the Energy Project found that employees who identify their work as meaningful are three times more likely to stay at their jobs and 1.4 times more engaged at work.[1] Unfortunately, many people usually wait for a tragedy or a challenging situation before they begin asking why in their lives and seeking to identify meaningful work. Meaning is measured by "the degree to which people find their work to have significance and purpose, the contribution work makes to finding broader meaning in life, and the desire and means for one's work to make a positive contribution to the greater good."[2] You can determine meaningful work by the degree that one's work fulfills the needs or aligns with one's beliefs and values.

A close cousin to meaning is *meaningfulness*. Jesper Isaksen, in discussing meaningfulness despite the type of work, states, "Meaningfulness is not an inherent characteristic of a specific type of work; it is an individual state of mind that occurs when an individual regards the relationships between him or herself and his or her context as satisfactory in some individually important way. People have an incomparably strong ability to construct meaning in even the most barren environments."[3]

Normally we don't see or hear meaning talked about in those terms. It's usually positioned as the best-case scenario, but researchers have found over and over again that a person can derive meaning in most situations he or she is in. *Meaningful work does not necessarily have to be preferred work.* Why is meaning important, anyway? You guessed right: for the benefits. No, I am not talking about those amazing employee benefits your human resources professional shared with you. I am talking about the benefits that meaningful work has for you.

Meaningful work does not necessarily have to be preferred work.

For starters, developing meaning in work decreases the likelihood of stress and boredom, and it positively impacts customer service. Workers who find their work filled with meaning beyond the financial benefits report higher satisfaction with their jobs, higher job performance, decreased stress, and longer tenure.[4] They report better psychological adjustment and possess qualities that most organizations seek. They also see their work as important. They appear more committed to their work, have less risk of turnover, and are more involved with the organization.[5] This is important to the worker but also to leadership and the organization.

Teresa Amabile and Steven Kramer analyzed creative work inside businesses and said, "Of all the things that can boost emotions, motivation, and perceptions during a workday, the single most important is making progress in meaningful work."[6]

People who feel their work is meaningless are more negative, feel more stressed, complain more, and feel more of a sense of hopelessness in their work. These workers tend to believe that meaning cannot be derived from their work, even if others were able to find meaning in the same role at the same company. Meaningless work is usually linked to burnout, apathy, and disengagement from one's work. We all want work to be meaningful!

There are also different levels of meaningful work. Lips-Wiersma describes four dimensions of meaningful work: (1) developing inner self, (2) unity with others, (3) service to others, and (4) expressing full potential.[7] No matter how you define meaningful work, when you have it based on self, others, and the organization, you have a winning combination. Have you been able to identify how your work is meaningful based on the above categories of self, others, and the organization?

How do you put this information into practice? One way to cultivate meaning is in relationships at work. Meaningful relationships are a vital part of meaningful work, which fosters positive community. Employees who are purposeful in pursuing these relationships increase their chances of growing and achieving at work while decreasing the chances of burnout. *People want to connect to work that is meaningful, and they want to connect to others at work in meaningful ways.* Both are important. You may be wondering, "How do I do this in a position, or a role, or a job that doesn't appear to foster meaning?" Another way to cultivate meaning at work is to craft your job.

CRAFTING YOUR JOB

Jake Kahut crafted his job to bring smiles to people's faces and create a positive work experience for those he encountered. He found a way to bring his Why to work to make a positive impact. He could have chosen to hate his job, but he chose to make his work a good experience.

There is somewhat of an unconscious cultural mandate to hate your job and to see it as merely an obligation to be fulfilled. If people believe that work can be enjoyable, it opens up the possibility that they might just enjoy it and craft experiences to help them fulfill this reality. This takes a sincere desire to want to see work differently, and it's not easy for many people. It's not simply about what you do but why you do it. Researchers found that people with jobs low on perceived prestige, including some jobs that were taken only out of financial necessity, can also approach work as calling and craft their jobs in ways that allow them to experience meaningful work and purpose.[8]

It's not simply about what you do but why you do it.

One study showed hospital cleaners engaging in work beyond their scope, like interacting with patients and visitors and timing their duties to be more efficient around nurses' schedules. "These employees enjoyed their work, felt their job tasks required a high degree of skill, and perceived their activity as critical in helping patients heal."[9] Another group of hospital cleaners did the exact same work, yet only saw themselves as cleaners and had a more negative perception of their work.

I saw something similar at my first job. I was a dishwasher at a retirement home when I was fourteen. I worked a job I wouldn't describe as overly exciting. I enhanced it by interacting with the residents and even ended up volunteering with one resident who was no longer able to tend the rose garden on the premises. This made me feel that my work was more meaningful. It didn't mean all of a sudden I loved doing the dishes, but it did mean I was able to "craft" my role in ways that made the work better and more meaningful. So what in the world is crafting anyway?

What Is Job Crafting?

Job crafting is defined as the "physical and cognitive changes individuals make in the task or relational boundaries of their work."[10] Job crafting is about creating or initiating change in a job instead of reacting or responding to a change in the job. It is where individuals proactively change the boundaries of their work in order to obtain more meaning from their work. An example of this is a custodian who thinks about her or his role as a way to provide the best possible learning environment for students in their classroom. He or she has changed the job cognitively to view it in a much more positive and meaningful light. Job crafting is ultimately something that is not seen or rewarded by others but creates an internal sense of meaning and value.

There are three main ways to job craft: (1) task crafting, (2) cognitive crafting, and (3) relational crafting. *Task crafting* involves changing a myriad of tasks within one's role, while *cognitive crafting* involves changing how one perceives his or her role. *Relational crafting* means changing who you interact with while you are performing your work. These actions impact the meaning of work and ultimately a worker's professional identity. Job crafting and personal initiative are similar in that initiative involves a level of self-starting and going beyond work duties. Job crafting has also been called by other names, such as "job enrichment" and even "task significance." No matter what you call it, there are practical implications for job crafting.[11]

Why Should I Craft My Job?

People tend to want to see themselves in a positive light, and work identity plays a role in how they view themselves. Most people want to do more than simply go to work to collect a paycheck. They want their work to count for something, to impact something, to ultimately mean something. There are three main reasons to job craft: (1) to gain a level of control over work, (2) to craft a positive self-image, and (3) to fulfill a need for connection with other people.[12] Gaining a level of control over work can be done through reframing, a technique used to describe or look at a situation in a different way. This technique works even in low-autonomy jobs, as evidenced by the research on the hospital cleaners who saw themselves as engaged in patient care. It is evident that they engaged in cognitive crafting as well as reframing their role in a way that was more meaningful.

Most people want to do more than simply go to work to collect a paycheck.

So far this sounds pretty good, right? Let's look at some of the benefits associated with job crafting:

- Feelings of doing worthwhile and meaningful work and an increased sense of purpose.
- Helps individuals take ownership of their engagement at work. It also helps them to have a positive outlook on their work experience.
- Improved self-image at work.
- Decreased absenteeism.
- Reduced turnover intentions, higher levels of engagement, higher performance, and employability.
- More connection and engagement with other people (coworkers and customers).
- Shifts the employee from a passive recipient of their work to a proactive participant with their work.

One study showed salespeople crafting their jobs, which was positively associated with higher-quality self-image, greater perceived control over work, and readiness to change.[13] Another study done on a Fortune 500 technology company showed that "engaging in job crafting led to short-term (six-week) boosts in happiness."[14] As you can see, there are many benefits of job crafting. Some people craft naturally and some don't.

How Do I Craft My Job?

At this point you might be thinking, "Okay, this is what I need. How do I do it?" Here are some practical ways:

- When a job may not appear that interesting, it can increase in meaning if there is understanding of why the task is important or necessary and ultimately how it plays a part in a larger purpose. Ask yourself how your job is important to you, your family, your teammates, or society in general.
- If an employee can see how her work contributes to achieving important organizational goals, she is more likely to see her work as meaningful and significant. The link between individual and organizational goals can be a powerful one. Identify ways that your specific work links to the organizational values (e.g., if you are a custodian at a school, you may find your work helps create a positive learning environment for the students who learn there).

Here are some examples of job crafting:

1. "When an internet service provider changes the framing of the work from being about making sales to being about connecting those who would otherwise be left behind in the computing revolution, the meaning of the work changes, as does the employee's identity (dealmaker versus champion of the masses)."[15]
2. Google instituted an infamous 20-percent-time declaration, where an employee could spend 20 percent of their time on a task or project that was meaningful to them. While it has been shared that it is no longer widely used, as Google continues to grow, there have been and continue to be some who take advantage of this crafting idea.

3. The job of a cashier has the potential to not be extremely rewarding, but some are able to craft their jobs by the level and type of customer service they provide, thus asserting a level of control over their interactions with the customer. You have met the type that act like they are mad that you walked in, haven't you? You have also met the type that amazed you with their upbeat personality, awesome smile, and second-to-none service!

4. I once worked in global human resources, and the role didn't give me those great goose bumps, but I remember volunteering to lead our team for the Susan B. Komen Race for the Cure. That one decision kept me engaged with the team and gave me a sense of identity, even if temporarily.

Risks of Job Crafting

Job crafting does come with risks. The dark side of job crafting is when job duties are changed by the employee to the extent that they go against organizational values or put the organization at risk, or even decrease the employee doing his or her "normally defined" role well. There is a reality of constraints to job crafting where one cannot go outside of his or her given structure.

In my early years, I worked as a training coordinator in the corporate training and development department of an organization. I felt unfulfilled partly because I had previously led a team of fifty people and now was leading a team of one: myself. I knew the shift to training and development was for me, but it was hard. In order to craft my role (I had no idea what I was doing then), I agreed to do a training for a friend within the same company on my off time. My manager received an email about what an amazing job I had done, but I was not rewarded. I was reprimanded. My role was not that of a trainer yet, and I had crafted my role in a way that put my department at risk. Please avoid my many mistakes!

While at that company, I grew in my career and came to what I now consider my calling. Now I get to live out my Macro Why most of the time.

JOB, CAREER, OR CALLING?

Do you have a job, a career, or a calling? The latter will give you the strongest sense of commitment and meaning. Job-focused people lean toward financial benefits, career-focused people lean toward career advancement, and calling-focused people lean toward enjoyment, fulfillment of their role, and knowing they are making an impact for the greater good. When you have a job, you may simply go to work and collect a check; when you have a career, you may feel like you have to find meaning in your work; but when you have a calling, you are intrinsically motivated and you love your work!

Calling can be defined as an overall purpose in one's work (greater good) and not necessarily day-to-day items. One benefit from approaching work as a calling can be seen in a study of education students who planned to go into teaching. The students in this study identified teaching as a calling, not merely a job or career. The students who approached their work as a calling displayed greater enthusiasm and commitment toward their careers as teachers, they were more mindful of their impact socially as teachers, and they were more likely to acknowledge their duties of teaching beyond the job description.[16] When an individual sees their work as a calling, they report greater work satisfaction, spend more discretionary hours working unpaid, have more faith in management, have greater vocational self-clarity, and have perceptions of their life having a greater meaning.[17] Another example of calling is what researchers call "sacred calling," when a person believes their occupation expresses the will of God in their work.

If your work doesn't feel like a calling, sacred or not, you are not off the hook. You can do work that you do not feel is your calling but incorporate items of meaning into your current role by job crafting. People who do this feel enjoyment and meaning in their current non-calling roles.

I would not advise what I am about to share. In one of my roles, I remember being so frustrated and so stressed that I was surely going to quit. I decided to challenge how I viewed the role and started to see it differently by thinking about the necessary skills I could develop within this role for my future (so far, so good!). Next, I created a logo of my future company and put it up in my cubicle as a reminder of why I was there. Needless to say, it is unwise to work for a company and put a logo of your future company up in your cubicle. I was politely asked to take it down, and I did. I could have put a picture of my logo in my pocket, or on my precious flip phone (remember those prehistoric items?), or even in my car. I had good intentions, but poor execution. Bless my little heart!

You may be wondering, "What if I have a difficult employer who doesn't allow me to escape the 'menial' tasks or does not give me room to craft my job?" I think you have to take ownership and make some tough decisions. You may consider volunteering in and outside of work, going back to school, or taking on a part-time job that is meaningful. Try to identify ways you can look at your job in a different light. If none of these options gets you to a better place, you may need to leave that role or the company (if that is realistically feasible).

You just finished part 1, my friend! You should have a better understanding of both your Macro Why and your Micro Whys and how to apply them in your life and at work. Your Why is unique to you, and you have the power to engage it and live a more fulfilling life at home and at work. While your Why is vital and important, if you do not do anything with it, it is relatively useless. Part 2 will help you to execute your Why with passion *now*! See you in part 2.

KEY TAKEAWAYS AND TIPS

p You do not only have to exhaustively try to find meaning in your work when you can also bring meaning to your work. Look for meaning in your work, and if it is lacking, look internally in order to bring meaning with you and make your work matter.

p One practical way to bring meaning to your work is to *craft* your role in such a way that you see how you and others are benefiting from it (training, bringing a smile to another person, helping a coworker, etc.).

p Identify meaning in your work by utilizing the "5 Why Bridges at Work" tool in Addendum C. This will help you identify what motivates you or can motivate you the most at work (e.g., Do you work for your family, team members, to make a difference in the community, etc.?).

p Do you have a job, career, or calling? The latter will ultimately lead to greater meaning at work for you. What will it take to either see your role as a calling or get you to a place where you are working in your calling?

Part Two

NOW:
Your Passion and Intensity

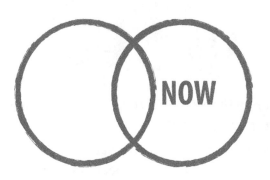

Don't wait.
The time will never be just right.

—Napoleon Hill

Chapter 6

ENGAGE:
Are You "On 10"?

David Lyons: High-Energy High School English Teacher and Mentor to Young Men

On the first day of twelfth grade, I sat in a new classroom, preparing for AP English. I'd heard about this teacher and his great energy and unique approach, but what I received that day and for the rest of the year went beyond anything I'd been told and had ever experienced. Mr. Lyons walked into the room with his hand raised, quickly moving it from side to side and doing a subtle little kick with his left leg. He would speak in a cadence that left you leaning on the edge of your seat, wondering what he would say next. He had the classroom sitting in a circle, and he danced around in the circle, making his inspiring points. These were the little quirks that made Mr. Lyons special. If you ever saw the movie *Dead Poets Society*, this was my Robin Williams, this was my "O

Captain! My Captain!" Mr. Lyons gave his all in class, and he was a mentor for young men who did not have strong relationships with their fathers. I was one of those young men.

Mr. Lyons's family inspired him, as he came from generation upon generation that worked hard, and it was passed down to him that "when you say you're going to do something, you do it with all your heart and you do it to the best of your ability." It amazed me that even at times when I and other students were at our worst, Mr. Lyons still found a way to reach us. In discussing some of us challenging students, he states, "There have been times when it would've been so much easier to fold it in, but my commitment, my mortal commitment, was to those children. It wasn't to the system, or the policies, or the ways that people who had not been in the classroom thought a classroom should be run. And when the children were harder for me to reach, it became my responsibility to go look in their records, to call the family, because I had to figure out how I was going to get into that kid's heart. It is really easy to just say, 'That's not worth it.' But by glory, it is always and will always be worth it." While other teachers may have been on autopilot, Mr. Lyons chose to act with passion and intensity.

Your Now is when you see this moment as important and you are ready to act with your best effort.

Passion is normally thought of as being passionate about what you do, or as some people ask, "Have you found your passion?" I have found this type of passion as a speaker and consultant, and I tell people all the time, "I would do this for free, but my kids won't let me." This is not the passion I am talking about in this section. I am talking about exerting passion, or in other words, effort and intensity, which is what I call the *Now*. Your Now is when you see this moment as important and you are ready to act with your best effort. Your Now is when you give your all. Another way I like to describe it is being "On 10." Mr. Lyons was a great example of what it means to be "On 10."

WHAT IS YOUR NUMBER?

Being "On 10" is a description I heard growing up. People said it when you gave 100 percent or when you were doing "too much." Being "On 10" can best be described through dancing. Before you roll your eyes, you might really like this example even if you don't like dancing. Have you ever been to an event where people are dancing, such as a wedding, a reunion, or someone's party? Normally there are three kinds of people there. There are the watchers and two types of dancers. The first type of dancer is calm, cool, and collected. When the music comes on, she calmly sways from side to side, uttering, "They're not going to see me sweat!" The second type of dancer lets the music come on and waits for that one special moment in the song where he goes all in! He is flailing all over the place, jumping up and down, and moving so fast that grandmas everywhere yell, "Stop!" You know this second type of dancer, don't you? Is she or he in the mirror? The first type of dancer is so concerned about what everybody else is doing and if they are looking her way. She is too concerned with how others are perceiving her. The second type of dancer doesn't care what people think and is leaving it all on the dance floor. He even brought three different undershirts because he knew he was going to sweat out each one. Which dancer do you think is "On 10"? Be that second dancer, and leave it all on the dance floor in your work and in life!

To be clear, I am not asking you to go to your next work meeting and flail with all you have, because your coworkers might call security. I am not asking you to go home and shake what your momma gave you, because your mother might tell you to stop shaking! However, I am asking you to be "On 10" in the sense of giving it your all. Identify what your unique best is for your work, and leave it all on the dance floor of your work and what matters most to you. Here are some questions to get you thinking about what it means for you to be "On 10," so you may want to bring out the piece of paper again.

"On 10" Questions

1. If you had to rate yourself today on how passionately you are living overall, how would you rate yourself on a scale of 1 to 10, with 10 being the most passionate? (There is always one comedian who yells out, "Eleven!" during my presentations. Please don't be that person, pretty please!)
2. What does it look like to be "On 10" at work and at home?
3. What are the attributes, behaviors, and actions of you being "On 10"?
4. What are the attributes of others who you feel are "On 10" (be mindful not to get caught in the comparison trap)?
5. When was the last time you felt "On 10" at work and at home? What were the contributing factors?

Don't be too high or down on yourself. If you rated yourself a 10 out of 10, realize that you can be a 10 in one place and a 4 in another. If you rated yourself a .001, first of all, you were supposed to use whole numbers, but you might be being a little hard on yourself. The fact that you are reading this book at all lets me know you aren't that low.

Processing Your 10

Here are some important things to consider as we process being "On 10." First, please avoid comparisons, because your 10 will be different from someone else's 10. When you are honest with yourself, you know exactly what you can give and what you can't. Some people give eighty hours a week at work on a regular basis, and you might not be able to do that with your new little baby, your special-needs child, or your aging parent who needs more of you these days. You have to be content with what you give while at the same time challenging yourself to give your very best!

Arati Desai Wagabaza challenges herself to be her very best. As the founder of tech start-up SmallCircles, she acknowledges the challenge in comparing her venture to the well-known tech companies—the Facebooks, Googles, and Ubers of the world. She reminds herself not to measure her growth and success by their success. This doesn't mean she doesn't set extremely high expectations, but she does it on her own terms and for her unique journey. In any industry, comparing ourselves to the front-runners would be a frustrating and daunting task. Arati says, "Why would I hold myself to that bar? If I do, then maybe suddenly I feel like I am failing!" We are wise to learn from Arati and avoid the comparison trap.

Second, in order to be "On 10," your 10 doesn't depend on anyone else. You don't need the perfect manager or perfect roommate or perfect dog to choose to be "On 10." It's what I call the Golden Rule of being "On 10!" Think of a time when you were served at a restaurant and expected excellence. You expected that server to be "On 10," and if she wasn't, you more than likely weren't thinking, "Well, maybe she has a bad manager, or maybe something happened at home, or maybe her little sweet puppy has a cold." You expected great service with a smile—no excuses!

You don't need the perfect manager or perfect roommate or perfect dog to choose to be "On 10."

What about your favorite artist or band? Growing up, mine was Michael Jackson! Whether you went to the concert and fainted or you fainted in front of your TV, you expected the three moves, didn't you? You expected the leg-kick thingy, the spin-around-really-fast move, and the moonwalk. What if Michael had come out onstage, brought a stool, and sung all his songs without dancing? You would have been disappointed, you would have been hurt, and you would have wondered why this body double was onstage and when the real MJ was going to skydive in. You expected him to be "On 10."

What about you? What fans at home and work are you disappointing by not doing your moonwalk? What prospective customers and clients are you letting down because you didn't bring your sparkly glove today? We expect a 10 from others; therefore, we should try our best to give ours. What's stopping you?

Regaining Your 10

At this point many people ask, "What if I've lost my 10? How do I regain it?" Here are some questions to help you work through why you lost your 10 and figure out how to get it back:

1. You first have to identify and know what your authentic 10 looks like. What does your best effort and intensity look like?
2. Did you allow your body double to perform for you? He or she can't do the moves like you, so why did you stop showing up to perform?
3. Have you allowed external situations to influence your internal fortitude? Who and what situation is weighing on you?
4. Are the people closest to you supportive of your 10? Who are you letting influence you?
5. Challenge yourself not to wait for the perfect situation to give your 10 performance. Who told you this present moment wasn't perfect and convinced you to wait for a future date?
6. Ask yourself, "What would my life be like, feel like, and look like if I operated 'On 10' on a more consistent basis?" What is stopping you from filling that gap?
7. Who is the one person that will challenge, encourage, and inspire you to be "On 10"? What are you waiting for? Call them, send them a message, Morse code them

if you have to, but let them know you need them now!
Your 10 depends on it.

8. Use the Four-Stage Analysis Model, or simply put, ask
   yourself the Four Questions: Where am I now? Where
   do I want to be? What are the barriers preventing me
   from getting there? How do I remove those barriers?

If you are honest in answering those questions, you will start to
understand where you are versus where you could be. Remember:
you can control your attitude, effort, and mindset no matter what
is happening externally.

HIGH VERSUS LOW NOW

When you have a High Now, you strive to be "On 10." You are
not as concerned about other people looking at you as long as you
know you're giving your very best. You understand that all these
little moments lead to bigger ones and that what you do right now
matters. When you have a High Now, you understand that the
people you surround yourself with are crucial to your development. A High Now can also be seen when a person no longer waits
for perfect. They aren't waiting for the perfect job, perfect manager,

perfect project, perfect family (this one will never come—trust me), or the perfect life. They realize that the "perfect" they are concerned with is the perfect moment to try, which is *now*.

A High Now can also be seen when a person no longer waits for perfect.

When you have a low Now, this moment doesn't really matter and you aren't concerned with how you are being influenced by others. A Low Now person is complacent and is okay with being "on 6" (no capitalization given on purpose). One practical way to be a High Now and "On 10" is to have real goals.

R.E.A.L. GOALS

Do you have goals? You can intend to do something, but an intention is not the same as a goal. Why are goals important? Goals help drive behavior by focusing attention, galvanizing energy, encouraging persistence, and facilitating strategy development. Ambiguous goals such as "I want to do better" do not work. What does "better" look like? It may look like, "I want to score a 10 out of 10 on improvement during my performance review." In order to be effective, your goals must be explicit and specific.

One example occurred for me in college. As an undergraduate, I had received several all-A report cards, and then I got one B+, making that 4.0 very elusive. I had only three semesters remaining, and I wanted to graduate with a 3.6 so I could graduate with honors. There were only eighteen classes left, so I knew I needed sixteen As and two Bs. The first semester I received six As. Woohoo! The second semester I received four As and two Bs. That was all the margin I had, and the last semester I received six As. My very specific but challenging goal increased my effort to obtain two 4.0 semesters. I worked hard!

The best goals are R.E.A.L. goals. Let me break that down for you. The best goals are ones that are Reachable, Explicit, Attractive, and Length-Conscious. Let's look at each of these characteristics and how each can help you live "On 10."

The best goals are ones that are Reachable, Explicit, Attractive, and Length-Conscious.

Reachable

Your goal should be reachable. It shouldn't be too simple, nor should it be too hard. Sometimes during my presentations, I do the unthinkable. I ask people to do something with their neighbor. I ask them to pull their neighbor's arm. What happens next is awesome. There are usually three different kinds of people. The first kind gently pulls the arm with an "I'm only doing this because he asked me to" attitude. The second kind are literally trying to tear the cartilage off the bone. The third is engaged in what I call the stretch zone. They are being stretched beyond their norm and they are stretching someone else. This is right where our goals should be. They should be reachable, but they should also stretch us beyond our normal.

Explicit

Explicit goals are goals that are very clear and specific. Studies have shown that people do better when an assigned goal is specific versus the "just do your best" type of assignment. Research also supports the notion that performance is enhanced when goals are both specific and challenging.

Attractive

Do you like things that are attractive? If for some reason you answered no, let me recommend a book on lying, because we all like things that are attractive. Now, what we deem attractive is different for everyone, but we do like attractive things, and we should state why our goal is attractive to us. How would it make you feel if you accomplished it? Some people find it helpful to visualize their goal and then go after it. One way this is talked about is with the term *goal intensity*, which is when one perceives his or her goal as important and commits to it. Are you clear on why your goal matters to you? Have you identified what makes it attractive to you?

Length-Conscious

Our goals should also have an end or deadline. They shouldn't go on forever. You shouldn't say, "I am going to get fit . . . one day." You also shouldn't say, "I am going to improve in my work ethic . . . at some point." This is something that you want to give an end, because goals are more effective when they have a deadline.

GOAL ACHIEVEMENT

There are several things to note when achieving more goals. First, Peter Gollwitzer's study on goal achievement found that telling other people your goals decreases your likelihood of accomplishing it, because you get a premature sense of accomplishment in what is called "social acknowledgement."[1] So, if you tell someone your goal, position it in a way that it can't be celebrated but that you will really have to work hard at it. For example, instead of sharing that you will run a marathon, share that you are starting to run, looking at shoes, running trails, and looking up future races in order to run a marathon in a year and overall get healthier. When we tie specific, immediate goals to larger, future goals, this will help us to achieve more goals.

When we tie specific, immediate goals to larger, future goals, this will help us to achieve more goals.

Second, we also should consider the challenges we will face in achieving our goals. When we think about the potential land-mines, it can help to avoid them. Heidi Grant Halvorson says, "It's not negative to think about the problems you are likely to face, but it is foolish not to."[2]

Sometimes the hardest part of achieving a new goal is simply getting started. Find the one thing that will get you started and moving in the right direction and is accomplishable. While an intern at a major beverage company, I took six other interns to Six Flags in my minivan (don't ask why a twenty-year-old had a minivan). Well, this little thing called gas somehow was no longer in my minivan, and the vehicle stopped. I learned a valuable lesson that day. No, it wasn't to always keep gas in your car. Sure, that's important, but it didn't resonate as the most profound. The most profound lesson for me was that the hardest part of starting is initially *getting started*. It was hard to start pushing that minivan, but once the wheels were in motion and we had momentum, it was so much easier. We were able to push that minivan to a safe area and eventually get some gas. What is that one thing that will begin to build momentum toward achieving your goals?

You need to not only believe you can achieve a goal, but grow in the skills to achieve it.

You also have to be open to learning new things to achieve your goals. *Believing you can achieve a goal is important, but believing you can grow in the range of skills necessary to achieve that goal is equally important.* Achieving your goals is vital to passionately pursuing your Why, Now! You are likely "On 10" when you are pursuing your R.E.A.L. goals with a relentless passion.

KEY TAKEAWAYS AND TIPS

p Being "On 10" means you are giving the very best that you can give that area in your life. How would you rate yourself on a scale from 1 to 10 (10 being the highest) in passionately living your Why?

p Avoid the "On 10" comparison traps. Someone else's 10 may be different from yours. Remember you're not achieving more as compared to other people, but to yourself. Are you progressing and challenging yourself to be better? Be challenged and encouraged by others, but remember we all have different priorities and values that lead to our 10.

p Identify what your "On 10" behaviors are, and try to just do one for a month to give more passion and effort.

p R.E.A.L. goals are Reachable, Explicit, Attractive, and Length-Conscious. When you frame your goals with these four items, you increase your chances of actually achieving them.

Chapter 7

FLOW:
Refocus, Recover,
and Recharge

Sowmya Murthy: Daughter, Business Coach, Chief Marketing Officer, and Adventurer

Sowmya was twenty-eight years old, working as a strategy consultant, and dating the man of her dreams. It suddenly all fell apart as he dropped a bombshell of news on her, saying, "I can't imagine having kids with you." She felt such shame and heartbreak and was determined to press on and never look back. What did she do next? She says, "I did what any hard-charging, alpha, twenty-eight-year-old female you could imagine that was about to go rule corporate America [would do]. I got right back on, and I took myself, some friends, and a backpack to Asia. Came back, went straight to my consulting gig . . . It looked like, 'That's Sowmya, nothing will knock Sowmya down.' Inside, the fire had already been lit. Why? Because until then I had not asked my 'Why.' I had perfected the art of 'how.'" That Asia trip ignited something in her. She would take three to four weeks off in reflection every year and go away by herself and practice the art of sitting with her discomfort. She would ask herself what problem she wanted to solve in her life. What issue had been zapping her of her energy? This was her yearly break and getaway to refocus, recover, and recharge! This is how she stayed in her zone to continue achieving more.

Have you ever heard someone say that they are in the zone, or that time stood still while they were playing a sport? Have you ever been doing something that you enjoy and you were fully engaged and wondered where all the time went? You may have been in the "flow," and in this chapter we will explore not only how being in the "flow" can help your passion and intensity, but also how energy, recovery, and sleep can help you to be "On 10!"

GO WITH THE FLOW

In 1975, Mihaly Csikzentmihalyi started his research asking why some people were highly motivated to do certain activities without stated external rewards, and he came up with the concept called "flow." Flow can be defined as undivided attention to a task, clear goals and feedback, perceived control over an activity, and the feeling of being exactly where you want to be in a moment. Csikzentmihalyi defined flow as "a psychological state in which the person feels simultaneously cognitively efficient, motivated, and happy."[1] It is when you feel your best and perform at your best. To make it practical: When was the last time that time stood still for you at work? What were you doing? What were you working on? What hobby were you engaged in? What made your work extremely enjoyable?

Flow is that special place where effort feels effortless. We have seen flow when Tiger Woods played in his prime, or when Michael Jordan made shot after shot after shot, or when Serena Williams played with amazing efficiency. You have also seen it when your favorite musician seemed to be locked in and gave her or his best performance. You may have seen it when NASA workers were preparing for a launch. You may have also seen it at work. True, deep, and intense flow experiences are rare and may only occur a couple of times in someone's lifetime. However, mini flow experiences can occur more often. Steven Kotler, director of the Flow Genome Project, says, "In flow, every action, every decision, arises seamlessly from the last. In this state, we are so focused on the task at hand that all else falls away. Action and awareness merge. Our sense of self vanishes. Our sense of time distorts. And performance goes through the roof."[2]

Flow is that special place where effort feels effortless.

Flow Benefits

Flow is generally found in the place where we are stretched but we do not snap. Not too easy and not too hard. In a flow state, individuals are being challenged and yet confident that things are in control. This balancing act makes it difficult to experience at times, but when you experience it, it is truly amazing.

Flow really can help you be "On 10." In a ten-year McKinsey study, managers who incorporated the flow concept shared that they were five times more productive in their flow experiences. If we could increase our flow experiences by 15 to 20 percent, McKinsey researchers suggest that our workplace productivity would potentially double. This is not just good research but also good science, according to Kotler, because five performance chemicals are released in our brains during flow: *norepinephrine* and *dopamine* help us to focus and increase with the importance of the goal, *endorphins* block out pain and allow us to accomplish more without burning out as fast, *anandamide* allows us to connect more thoughts and insights, and *serotonin* prompts us to feel good and create a better bonding experience with others. Flow also helps us to limit or minimize distractions, have more creative ideas, make quicker connections between ideas, and find easier workarounds. It inspires learning and challenging tasks.[3]

You might be able to get into flow even in a job that you do not consider your Why job. One way to do this is by seeing a duty or identifying something specific you do that drives great meaning for you. If you are able to do that duty without many distractions and with focus, you might just achieve a flow experience. You do not have to have your dream job to have a flow experience. You just need your dream attitude to see how this can help you and/or others and be challenged in a way that drives you toward progress.

Flow Environment

"So how do you have flow?" you might ask. Or better stated, "How does one practically create an environment where flow is more likely to happen?" Here are three practical ways: (1) Do something that stretches you or your skill set (not too simple and not too hard); (2) care about what you are doing, and see it as something that matters and will add value; and (3) focus on the task at hand (limiting interruptions and distractions). Flow is attached to our Why and the meaning it carries for us. It is also attached to our ability. Our perceived skill level or ability is important with flow. For example, it is unlikely I will currently "flow" with the Rubik's Cube because I have no idea what I am doing, perceive my ability to be very low, and honestly don't have a desire to learn it. Flow is still valuable if the importance of the task is high, even if skill exceeds the level of difficulty. It is important to note that research has found that flow is more applicable for individuals who have high-achieving behaviors or have a hope for success. Flow is also impacted by our energy. If you want to achieve flow, it's important to be aware of and manage your energy.

MANAGE YOUR ENERGY

What gives you energy? What keeps you going throughout the day? And no, I am not talking about the gallons of coffee that you might drink. I'm also not talking about the daily drinks that give you energy (you know who you are). Human energy is like a battery in that it can be depleted throughout the day; therefore, it is important to manage it. Can you relate to the following? "I've habitually spent my days immersed in projects, poring over details, and running from one engagement to another without a break—and it's suffocating! I've even gone so far as to hold my urge to use the bathroom all day so I could make one more phone call, one more meeting, or one more something."[4] One great way to manage our energy is through recovery.

It is important that we understand the difference between rest and recovery. Rest can include doing something not work-related. It is the absence of doing work, but it could include getting angry at politics or stressed about an important decision. This rest is not recovery because the brain has not had a chance to have a break from its high arousal state. It's like being a construction worker who uses his or her arm all day and then goes to the gym to have "arm day." You may have rested, but you did not recover. Recovery is recharging and allowing yourself to be refueled.

Benefits of Recovery and Dangers of Not Recovering

Caleb Asomugha is a sixth-grade special education teacher in New York. He looks like a bodybuilder, as Caleb takes working out very seriously. He told me, "You cannot be excellent if you're not taking care of yourself, and I remind myself about that daily. There were times when I would burn it on both ends and just find myself not being able to give as much as I wanted. I realized that there are some nonnegotiables that I have in my life in order for me to be excellent, in order for me to give my best to my colleagues and my kids. These nonnegotiables are gym time. I have to have gym time. I have to stay fit to perform at an optimum level physically and mentally. I have to have a vibrant spiritual life, so I have to stay on top of that. Then, emotionally, I just have to be there emotionally, so I have to have a couple of meetups with friends a week in order to stay in tip-top shape." With the hard work that Caleb must do to inspire the next generation of children, rest and recovery are important.

Lack of recovery dramatically holds you back from being resilient and successful. What impedes the recovery process is doing something that engages the same process that one would do during work. It is like an IT professional fixing a computer crash at home or for friends.

Lack of recovery dramatically holds you back from being resilient and successful.

At the end of the day, what can help us effectively recover? One way is not thinking about work during nonwork times, as this is associated with psychological recovery. There really are benefits to not thinking about work, as it has been demonstrated that those who are able to detach psychologically from work during evening hours reported a more positive mood and less fatigue at bedtime than those who consistently thought about work at those same times. When you do not unplug from work, and when you don't unplug the right way, you are giving yourself very little chance to recover before the next day. Not only that, but many people have a "second shift" that involves family, roommates, and child care when they finish their workday. Positive unwinding and recovery from work stress during workday evenings is associated with higher energy, higher work engagement, and positive behavior the following workday.

Working long hours or overtime may be associated with poor recovery, including not being able to relax at home and having low sleep quality.[5] It's not only working long hours that can hurt you, but what you do on the weekend matters as well. Research shows that recovery experiences on the weekend positively relate to joviality and lower levels of fatigue at the end of a weekend. So what can you practically do to help in your recovery efforts?

Practical Recovery Tips

Here are several tips that can help with recovery. Focus on one or two that make the most sense to you, and consistently build habits around them.

1. Recover internally by taking short breaks, shifting attention, and changing tasks when mental or physical resources for your primary task are low or gone (we'll talk about this more next).
2. Use an app that can help, like Unplugged, or put your phone in Airplane mode or DND (Do Not Disturb).
3. Don't have lunch at your desk, but walk around the office, get out of the office, go on a walk, or take someone out to lunch.
4. Engage in activities such as socializing with friends and conversation with family, which can lead to recovery because of the possibility for social support.
5. Physical activity and exercising can lead to recovery because they increase the release of endorphins and lead to enhanced secretion of noradrenalin, serotonin, and dopamine, all of which have antidepressant effects. This leads to positive psychological benefits because a person can not only detach from work but increase his or her sense of belonging if working out in a group.
6. Minimize working on off time, as it has been shown to lead to daily recovery declines. Working out daily during nonwork time has led to higher daily recovery levels for employees, especially those who may be considered workaholics.
7. If you are experiencing little to no meaningful work, then job craft, develop a meaningful hobby, and/or join

an organization. If you have a lack of social support, then intentionally connect with family and friends. If you are just tired, then watch your TV favorite show. Just don't binge watch daily unless it's old episodes of *The Office* (that's what they said!).

8. Like Sowmya, take your annual vacation, because it has been shown by *Business Insider* that not taking an annual vacation is associated with bad health, decreased productivity, and being bad for our relationships.[6] It really shouldn't be this hard to convince you to take those days.

While recovery is one way to manage your energy and maintain your capacity to be "On 10," taking breaks is another way to give your best Now. I know it seems counterintuitive that taking breaks exhibits a focus on the Now, but trust me (and the break experts)—this next section will show how breaks help maximize your Now by maximizing your energy.

Breaks

One extremely important area in work is something that I have personally seen and experienced take a hit in recent years, and that has been the power of a break. No, this is not a return of the old-school dance, but something that has the potential to also be old-school. It is almost seen as a weakness if you take breaks in some organizational cultures. I have seen companies applaud those who work and eat lunch at their desks regularly, and I have also seen schools take away precious planning time for teachers (this was not really a break, though).

Breaks at work are necessary because internal recovery can occur from short rest breaks (coffee or lunch), as they manage fatigue and help to maintain performance. Frequent ten-minute breaks with flexibility and strength routines can decrease anger, fatigue, and depression.[7] However, here is one thing that you should not do when you break. You should not do a chore during break time (I hear both gasps and applauding at that line). Here is why: you are less likely to recover when doing chores for a break, but when you socialize, nap, and relax, it leads to better recovery and performance than chore breaks (working with clients, running errands, and preparing for upcoming meetings).

So what are some helpful break-time activities? One study showed more positive associations with vitality and energy occurred when participants used their break times to learn something new, focus on what gave them joy at work, set a new goal, do something that made a colleague happy, show gratitude to someone they work with, seek feedback, reflect on how they make a difference at work, and reflect on the meaning of work.[8] Try incorporating some of these activities into your breaks and notice the difference in your recovery.

There is a dark side to breaks, and that is if they are frequent or last for a long time. This can lead to disengagement and require a longer start-up period to reconnect with the task at the same level as before the break. Your manager may also notice and ask where you have been for your four-hour lunch (yikes)! To avoid the dark side and have a good break life, consider scheduling some break times with distinct start and end times. When I interned on the marketing team at Coca-Cola, the team scheduled time every week to go into an eclectic room and just think, ponder, and brainstorm to get new ideas and concepts for branding. I loved this time!

If you consistently don't take breaks, don't take vacations, and don't take lunches, then my friend, you will experience one word: burnout!

Burnout

Burnout generally results from an unfavorable work environment with high demand on low resources and can be measured by exhaustion and being disengaged (lack of interest) in one's job.

There are several burnout indicators: low social support from manager and colleagues, cynicism, irritability, perceived helplessness toward work, decreased meaningful interactions, and no/limited recovery or breaks.

If you do not take breaks, lunches, and vacations, you will likely experience burnout.

One study showed that employees who were low in burnout (exhaustion and disengagement) showed relatively little difference in their physical vigor when doing work during off time. However, those who were high in burnout had less physical vigor when doing work during nonwork times.[9] This means that if you are at burnout or close to it, you may want to reconsider doing work during off time because you will not be able to give your maximal effort. The study shows that socializing was a great recovery for burnout, and that individuals experiencing high-risk levels of burnout should start doing more low-effort recovery (e.g., watching TV, resting, nothing). What is intriguing is if you are not at risk of burnout, low-effort activities don't really help you. Therefore, you can skip your many daily hours of TV watching and recover more efficiently. One thing that was helpful for all of the employees in the study, regardless of risk of burnout, was physical activity. So exercise and recover well, my friends. Stay away from burnout, and get some sleep (or at least a nap here and there).

GET YOUR ZZZZZS

This next section is all about sleeping and naps (yawn) to help you unleash your Now. Without the proper recovery and rest, you cannot effectively be "On 10." I know you may feel you don't have time for this, you need to be more productive, and you need to do something now. As I engaged the research about operating with great passion and intensity, I was a little bored with this area as well, but I have seen the benefits in my own life and in numerous wonderful studies, including ones I will share in this section. I have seen that it's not how hard you work, but how smart you work, and it is smart to get sleep and take intentional naps.

Is this your slogan: "Lunch Is for Losers and Sleep Is for Slouchers"? It is almost seen as a badge of honor to get little to no sleep. In her book *The Sleep Revolution*, Arianna Huffington says, "We sacrifice sleep in the name of productivity, but ironically, our loss of sleep, despite the extra hours we put in at work, adds up to more than eleven days of lost productivity per year per worker, or about $2,280."[10] Do you see how important sleep is now? That is roughly 2,280 items at the dollar store.

Benefits of Sleep

Sleep is important. It decreases health disorders, sick leave, work interruptions, all-cause mortality, and safety concerns. Adequate and efficient sleep is a key factor in productivity. A study of airline crews saw a decrease in operational performance and an increase in errors with crew members who had less than six hours of sleep in the twenty-four hours before work.[11]

So how much sleep should we really get? The general rule fluctuates now between seven and eight hours of sleep. This is different for everyone, as some people will only sleep for six hours and others far less. No matter your current low-hours sleep pattern, our bodies need to be retrained to sleep, even if that means getting to bed earlier.

Another area of focus is weekend sleep. Weekend sleep has also been shown to be a great time to recover. I know, I know. You look at this and say, "Yeah, right! This cannot and does not happen because of four letters: K-I-D-S!" This is a tough one, but if you are able to think of small and practical ways to get back some of that sleep, it can help you. Maybe a little less social media, TV time, or even reading this book for the eighth time (I wish). Whatever you do, prioritize your sleep, because your Now is dependent on it.

Benefit of Naps

I think most people agree that sleeping is good for you, but there is disagreement on napping. Most people who take naps feel physically awesome, but many also feel guilty for the "time lost" throughout the day. Let's dig in a little more.

Napping has normally been perceived as negative, but it may be quite good for you and your energy. Harvard University has shown that napping is good for everyone by helping with recovery and performance, but naps are especially helpful for night-shift workers, health care workers, international airline pilots, truck drivers, and even knowledge workers. They found that napping boosts creativity, alertness, performance, mood, and productivity.[12] Several companies have gotten on board with this idea and created a culture that is nap-welcoming, like Huffington Post, Google, Ben & Jerry's, and Zappos, to name a few. The Harvard researchers found that an hour-long nap at work led to computer programmers writing better code. They also concluded that even a short nap, less than an hour, can lead to better processing of information. The twenty- to thirty-minute naps revive and refocus workers.[13] NASA conducted a study with the Federal Aviation Administration and looked at commercial pilots in long-haul flights (longer than eight hours). The pilots in the rest group, who took naps, maintained consistent performance. Pilots in the no-rest group saw several pilots fall asleep. They found that in only twenty-six minutes of actual sleep (they tried to nap for forty minutes), the rest group pilots improved cognitive performance by 34 percent and alertness by 54 percent.[14]

Napping has normally been perceived as negative, but it may be quite good for you and your energy.

So here are some practical ways you can get a few winks. First, utilize nap rooms if your office has them, and if it does not, you can use my makeshift nap room—the car or a quiet space in the office.

Set your alarm on your phone, and if you are like me, make it very loud and out of reach so you actually have to get up and turn it off, so you don't turn it off in your sleep and come back to work a little later than expected (this happened to a "friend"). Aim for fifteen to thirty minutes, because that's how long most breaks are, but you don't want to go too long past an hour or it messes up your sleep schedule, and you may wake up more tired than before your nap.

This can be a tough one to absorb because we have been told for so long that breaks and naps are evil, but they are proving to be helpful for not only our work productivity but also our creativity. This book has benefited greatly from my naps, as I have been able to be more creative and alert, and to process more information faster when I have taken a short nap in the middle of the day.

GENERAL RECOVERY TIPS

So you've learned about flow, managing your energy and recovery, and getting good sleep. Here are some additional tips to help you refocus, recover, recharge, and work smarter:

Tip 1: Understand your ultradian rhythm, and no, this is not some calculus problem. Ultradian rhythms are the 90- to 120-minute interval cycles where we transition from a high-energy state to decreased energy. A study of Berlin Academy of Music violinists showed that those who practiced for ninety minutes and took short breaks and naps were better than the violinists who practiced all the way through with few or no breaks.[15] We need to seek recovery every 90 to 120 minutes because our glucose and blood pressure levels drop. When we don't seek recovery, our capacity to perform decreases. Take short, focused breaks and recover. Eat something, drink something (water preferably), move around (go for a walk around the office or outside), call a friend to just say hello, watch a motivational video, or write a thank-you note. Ultimately, you have to find what works for you.

Tip 2: Find a work/break method that works for you. The Pomodoro technique focuses on working in bursts, or what some call sprints, that are generally twenty minutes at a time with a short break. There are a lot of apps that will even count the time for you and alert you when it is time to break and get back to work. The ninety-minute work interval with ten- to fifteen-minute breaks in between works for those long sessions and may create a better flow environment, or the classic 50/10, which is fifty minutes of work with a ten-minute break. Try one that you think will work for you and your specific work and implement it for a month, then evaluate if that particular break method works for you. What I have found is that the best method for me depends on what I am doing. Sometimes working for ninety minutes and taking a fifteen-minute break when I have longer periods to work, and sometimes working for fifty minutes and taking a ten-minute break works better when I have shorter periods to work.

Tip 3: Find a place where you can work uninterrupted on a challenging project or assignment. The more challenging the project, the fewer interruptions (both internal and external) you need. When you try to multitask, it can increase the amount of time necessary to finish a primary task by 25 percent. Think about how often you may get email interruptions. Identify two or three times a day when you can check and respond to email, but try not to let this be the first thing you do.

Tip 4: Focus! I want you to do a silly but important exercise. Focus on something right in front of you and keep your eyes focused on it. Now, put your hand in front of your face and move it from side to side in front of you as fast as you can, but keep your focus on that object. Are you still able to see the object? What did your hand look like? If you were moving it fast enough, it should have looked like a blur because you were focused on the object. You stay connected when you're focused on something, no matter how many things threaten to distract you. (Important note: Do not do this exercise when your manager or an office guest is walking by, or it might be on your annual performance plan as "employee dancing wildly at work." Just saying!)

> It's not the hours we sit at the desk that matter, but
> rather the effort we give at the desk.

Ultimately, it's not the hours we sit at the desk that matter, but rather the effort, energy, and focus we bring to the time we are at that desk. It's like asking the question, "Do you go to the gym, or do you go to the gym and work out?" I know a lot of people who go to the gym, fewer who work out, and even fewer who work out with great effort. Don't go to the gym and lounge around or work out hard with bad form. Work out with great focus, form, and intensity. Don't simply go to work, but go to work with great form, and work with great focus and intensity. This can be accomplished with adequate amounts of rest, recovery, and working in "flow"!

KEY TAKEAWAYS AND TIPS

p One way to accomplish more and be more productive is to have a flow experience. A flow experience is when you are locked in, focused, and fully engaged in an activity or task.

p You can create an environment where flow is more likely to occur by limiting interruptions, caring about what you are doing, and being slightly stretched in your ability.

p Practical ways to recover are to take breaks, take your lunch (away from your desk), and periodically change up the tasks you focus on.

p If you are experiencing high levels of burnout, you may benefit from positive social interactions, physical activity, and taking time to do absolutely nothing.

p You can accomplish more when you are well-rested (sleep and naps). Practice recovery and find a work rhythm that makes sense for you and your working conditions.

Chapter 8

SHIFT:
Kick Normal Out the Door

Jess Ekstrom: Founder and CEO of Headbands of Hope

As an eighteen-year-old college student, Jess worked a summer internship with an organization that grants wishes to children with life-threatening illnesses. She would sadly watch these little kids lose their hair while being treated with chemotherapy. These kids weren't really worried about covering up their heads after their hair loss, but they wanted something they could wear to restore their self-confidence. Jess always saw them wearing headbands. She started looking for a company that provided headbands to kids with cancer, but she couldn't find one. An idea was birthed, and she shifted from being a normal college student to being an extraordinary one by creating this organization as a way to donate headbands to children with cancer. She says, "I saw a need, so I was going to create a solution!" This passion has led her headbands to appear in more than one thousand stores and impact hundreds of thousands of individuals, as she donates one headband to a child with cancer for every headband that is purchased. Jess has abandoned any semblance of normal in this noble pursuit.

When you have a High Now, doing enough is not good enough.

Have you ever accepted being normal, simply fitting in, and conforming to the norm? It can be so easy to simply "mail it in" or just do enough to get by, but when you have a High Now, doing enough is not good enough. In order to challenge "normal," you must challenge your cruise control, become more mindful, and continue to develop a learning mindset.

CHALLENGE YOUR CRUISE CONTROL/AUTOPILOT

Too many people settle for normal or average. Too many people are just existing and showing up to work or getting started at home without giving their all. I have encountered too many small business owners who are not giving their best effort. To be fair, I have been one of those people who has just existed and followed the plan of normal. I didn't like my results, and I hope you don't/ didn't either. Sometimes this happens when we press cruise control in our lives. If you have a car or have ever driven a car, have you ever pressed the cruise control button? What happens next? If you are like many people, you may take off your shoes, turn up the music, pull out that phone and make some calls, braid your hair, put on your makeup, play sudoku (well, maybe not braid your hair). We tend to relax, get comfortable, and shift from active driver to somewhat of a passive driver. We are still driving, but not with the same focus and effort we used when we had to press the gas pedal to go.

Another analogy for "coasting" this way is being on autopilot.

Let me be honest with you—I have never flown a plane, so I can't factually tell you what happens when you do, but I have some friends who are pilots, and I can also share my research with you. There are some real negative effects of autopilot. When using autopilot, pilots spend more time mind-wandering, where they sit and stare versus being in an active role.[1]

What's amazing is that we do this with our lives at work and at home. We get comfortable and kick up our feet. We start getting into the routine of "normal." Let's change that! Most people are on a consistent pattern of repeat. Is what you are repeating helping or hurting you when it comes to giving great effort and passion? What can you do to keep your work challenging and your life spicy, in order to keep cruise control off and autopilot deactivated?

As a national media personality and chief operating officer of I Call Her Queen, LLC, Faraji Muhammad has several tips for challenging your autopilot. In our interview he shared, "When you are in that place of autopilot, check your surroundings. It might be the people that you're with, or it might be the actual physical environment that you're in." He went on to say, "The people that are highly successful, they have to make some very, very serious and concrete decisions from the very beginning. One of the biggest decisions they had to make was determining who they were surrounded by." I agree with Faraji in challenging who surrounds us, and I also think we should sometimes challenge what we do in our everyday lives.

One thing I do every birthday is challenge myself to do something that I have never done by the next birthday. The first year I tried this, I challenged myself to run a marathon. I didn't run one. So I tried it again and said by the next year I would run my first marathon, and I did. Well, I mostly ran my first marathon. There was some serious fast walking going on at times. This past year I said I would go skiing or snowboarding for the first time, and I was able to join some good friends of mine who went to Vail, Colorado, and went skiing. I am so happy I fulfilled this year's desire. I am still trying to figure out what next year is going to be, but I am planning to climb Mount Kilimanjaro in Tanzania in two years. Setting these goals allows me to consistently challenge myself and not get locked into cruise control or the routine of normal. What about you? What can you do to challenge yourself every year or every birthday? It's what I call the *Birthday Challenge*. Will you take it? (Move your head up and down.)

Mindfulness and Mindlessness

Another way to challenge cruise control and engage in a High Now is to have a state of mindfulness instead of mindlessness. I am not asking you to go somewhere and cross your legs and breathe deeply for six seconds (even though I love the breathing exercises). I am encouraging you to be present in the moment. To take it all in at work and at home. To notice the people around you. To notice the person in the mirror. To see the expressions on your roommate's face or your family's faces. To notice and talk to the attendant at the gas station or the cleaner in your building. Mindfulness is defined as a feeling of engagement or involvement. Its benefits are an increase in competence, positive affect, creativity, and reduced burnout.

Mindlessness is an inactive state of mind that relies on how you have already defined an interaction or experience in the past. Most people do not notice mindlessness in themselves, even though they can see it clearly in other people. Mindlessness can be prevalent in us sometimes when we have a single point of exposure or rote repetition in a task or with a person. The single point of exposure happens when people hear or read something and just accept it without questioning it. Let me ask you this: What side of the street should cars drive on? You are right. It depends on what country you live in. In India, Australia, and Ireland, they would naturally say the left. In the United States and Canada, they would naturally say the right. Let me ask you another question. What side of the sidewalk should we walk on? In the United States, people will generally agree on the right, but why have we generally accepted the norm? While I believe there are truths that are not relative, many people operate in mindlessness behavior.

Most people don't notice their own mindlessness, though they see it clearly in others.

Let me show you where mindfulness and mindlessness can be best seen. Have you ever bought something new, maybe a new car, purse, or jacket, all of a sudden you begin noticing that car, purse, or jacket a lot more? You ask yourself, "Did everyone copy me?" Those items were generally there all along, but you didn't notice them because you weren't looking for them. What's sad is that many people aren't noticing that they are living on cruise control and autopilot. This also plays out in conversations with people as they process events and their lives. As the saying goes, "People are often in error, but seldom in doubt."

Mindfulness or mindlessness can be seen in how we talk about things and frame things. Why is that important? How we frame things can potentially destroy our creativity and innovation. In a 1987 study, Alison Piper and Ellen Langer introduced people to an ambiguous object in either an absolute (is) or conditional (could be) way. They said the object was a dog toy to one group (absolute) and could be a dog toy to another group (conditional). They then created a need for an eraser, and the only people who thought to use the object as an eraser were the ones told "it could be" a dog's toy. Those who were told it was a dog's toy didn't even think to use it as an eraser.[2]

This reminds me of a painful place in my education history. I had one of the biggest tests in my life, my kindergarten entrance test for public school. My mom tells me that I answered all the questions perfectly until we arrived at the request that I show them the brush not on the table. There were two brushes. One brush was on the table and the other was not on the table. Guess which one I picked up? The one on the table. I picked up the brush and showed it to them "not on the table," but I was marked wrong. Fortunately, they still let me in, but to this day my mom protests their scoring was wrong. Even then I was challenging the boundaries of what people believe is possible. Mom, I agree with you. I was right!

How are you framing things? Are you framing things like "This is how I am supposed to work," or "Most people don't love their jobs, so why should I think I could?" or "Why try so hard when everyone else isn't?" That's normal, and remember we are kicking normal out the door. Normal, see you later, because you have to go! Bye, Felicia! (If you didn't get that one, search the Internet for it.)

Practical Tips

Here are a few practical tips to help you challenge your cruise control, kick normal out the door, and engage your Now!

Tip 1: Take initiative and go beyond normal requirements. What can you do beyond your normal job description? What idea may help your team or organization innovate and grow? I remember my first temp job working for the American Red Cross as a recruiter for phlebotomists (trust me: I also had no idea what that was until I started recruiting them). They are the kind people who prick your veins at a blood drive (I just made you 1,000 percent smarter). This job wasn't particularly challenging for me, but I needed a job. I hadn't finished school yet, and as I began to learn the Red Cross organization, I came up with a concept to create a college competition to raise the most blood donations (insert creepy vampire joke here). I shared it with my manager, and she shared it with the executive director. She wanted me to share it with him, so I did. Well, I didn't last in that job a long time, but when I left I was invited to be a part of the board of directors for that region (the youngest member, I might add). I went from temp to board member. It took initiative. Now, don't applaud me too loudly, because there have been *many* instances where I have failed to take initiative and I have accepted the routine of normal. But my Why is inspiring me to do that less and less. What about you?

Where can you be more mindful and take great initiative at work or at home to kick normal out the door?

Tip 2: Conduct a quarterly or monthly Plus/Delta with your professional stakeholders (key team members, employees you lead, your manager). A Plus/Delta simply asks two questions. Plus: What am I doing well? and Delta: What do I need to change or improve? It is something I learned at one of my most challenging employment experiences, but it is something I use in my presentations, consulting, and even personal life. You do not have to wait for your professional stakeholders to come to you and ask these questions, but be proactive and seek out their feedback. People who want to grow seek out feedback on how they can improve. Normal people wait for it or only ask for the good feedback. Be anything and everything but normal. Be weird!

INTERRUPTING INTERRUPTIONS

Allow me to introduce you to an amazing stay-at-home mother and homeschooler, Maryjane Lueck. One of the unique ways that she is able to lead a disciplined life is by the red circle she puts on her door every day. Yes, this is a makeshift stop sign that signals to the kids and adults in the neighborhood when to not knock on the door because school is in session. While I have experienced some mediocre homeschoolers, Maryjane is definitely not mediocre. With her insightful way to challenge disruptions, she has created a space for her and her kids to focus, concentrate, and achieve more.

How many interruptions do you have a day? How many buzzes, calls, email dings, social media rings, doorbell ringing, kids crying, dog barking, coworker talking interruptions do you have a day? I only listed the external interruptions, but there are the internal kind too. Internal interruptions are mind-wandering, daydreams, intrusive thoughts, and spontaneous cognitive thoughts. Another name for internal interruptions is self-interruptions. Did you know that 40 percent of task switching (stopping one task and doing something else) is due to self-interruptions?[3] A whopping

40 percent! Now lay on top of that the external interruptions, and you see why it is lowering the Now of many people. In 2006, it was found that most people have email continuously running in the background and switch to check email about every five minutes.[4] This number has probably increased by now.

The average person engages with his or her phone 76 times every day. These distractions could account for more than two hours of time.[5] *Harvard Business Review* reported, "One workplace study found an average of almost 87 interruptions per day (an average of 22 external interruptions and 65 triggered by the person himself). Then, on average, it takes over 23 minutes to get back on task after an interruption, but 18 percent of the time the interrupted task isn't revisited that day."[6]

Our inner thoughts are also constant interrupters of us being in the moment. For example, thinking about weekend activities consistently while at work can lead to boredom and negative thoughts at work, but consistently thinking about your work meeting tomorrow while at home can lead to being less interested with conversations at home. It is time for interruptions to be interrupted.

One big interruption that many people do not see, but is nonetheless harmful, is multitasking.

One big interruption that many people do not see, but is nonetheless harmful, is multitasking. I'm sorry to tell you—while multitasking may appear to work, it really doesn't allow you to do multiple things with great focus, effort, and intensity. A study was done where people were asked to perform tasks from more than one role, for example, work and family, in a thirty-minute period. This resulted in reduced task enjoyment, negative mood, and distress. Going back and forth decreased the participants' engagement.[7] Multitasking does not work, as performance degrades when attention is divided, especially during complex tasks. What's interesting is that people multitask more when they feel negatively toward the task (frustrated, stuck, or bored).[8] Once and for all, we must focus on the task in front of us and stay locked in as best we can until we achieve the task, or at least focus for the allotted time we give it. Yep, you got it: no "On 10" to be found in multitasking.

Practical Tips

Here are a few tips to help you interrupt interruptions and stay "On 10."

Tip 1: You've heard the phrase "Eat the Frog First"? That means engage the hardest or most challenging task of the day first thing. Don't check email or listen to voicemail first thing if you can help it, unless your most challenging task involves checking email. This will take you down rabbit holes, and you will put off the big things you need to do more immediately.

Tip 2: Have somewhere to put your thoughts when they invade your mind. Internal interruptions can disrupt your flow and cause you to lose momentum in your current task if you do not put them somewhere, like a sticky note, or your calendar, to address them later. This is why many people find David Allen's *Getting Things Done* attractive, as it advocates for having a place for those thoughts and ideas to go.

Tip 3: Engage in interruption batching, which is when you group potential interruptions together (i.e., office hours, or predetermined times to check email or voicemails). This can help minimize the negative effect they can have on important projects or task momentum.

CONTROL WHAT YOU CAN CONTROL

What can you control? You guessed right: yourself. That is it. You can try your hardest to control everything else. If you have kids, you know or will soon find out that you can influence them but you can't control them. What's frustrating is that we spend so much time trying to control others and then wonder why they still choose to do something else. It's time to focus on our internal locus (Dr. Seuss and Stephen Covey would be so proud!).

Locus of control can be described as both internal and external. It is internal if a person believes that they have control based on their responses, skills, and abilities. External locus of control sees things as unrelated to behavior and attributes things to luck, chance, or something else external. A person who feels they are not in control, whether real or perceived, will not try as hard because they believe the outcome is independent of their effort or ability. This is somewhat of a learned helplessness. When you have an internal locus of control and self-responsibility, you generally are more motivated to achieve more successful outcomes.

We should focus on what we can actually control.

We should not minimize the impact of external forces, but we should still focus on what we can control. Sometimes our ideas will not be valued, sometimes our effort is not seen, but we should focus on what we can control. Everything else will lead to more frustration. Those who have more of an internal locus of control also tend to have more of a learning mindset.

THE LEARNING MINDSET

When you develop the learning mindset, you will be able to give greater effort, be more productive, and overcome obstacles more readily. This mindset can help minimize the self-destructive thoughts we may process about ourselves and our work and frees us to work and live more passionately! Growing in the learning mindset has helped me to process things differently, focus on the right part of tasks, and apply great action now. I believe that as you embrace the heart of the learning mindset, it will do these things for you too.

Are you more learning oriented or more performance oriented? Let's look at what that means as we explore the learning mindset.

Task Involvement versus Ego Involvement

When you are task involved, you focus on mastery and learning, versus when you are ego involved, you focus on performance as compared to other people. Task involved: improvement is the goal, learning is the focus, and people feel more intrinsically motivated. Ego involved: people feel less able when high effort is needed. Those who are ego involved perceive that high effort means you have low ability. Have you noticed in society that we prize people when they make things look easy, but when people show great effort, it is not prized as highly? Task-involved people see effort as a means to learning, mastery, and increasing their ability. Ego-involved people view failure as an indicator of low ability and thus shy away from likely failure. Having a learning mindset means being more task involved, which focuses more on learning, intrinsic motivation, and improving overall.

Learning Goals versus Performance Goals

There is a difference between learning and performance goals. Learning goals focus on feedback as data points to continue to improve, whereas performance goals focus on feedback as points to identify one's current level of ability. Individuals who mainly use learning goals see performance outcomes as more internal, controllable, and changeable according to effort levels (i.e., I can achieve more if I give more effort). Individuals who mainly use performance goals view performance outcomes as internal but unchangeable, whereas effort might be increased but it implies lower ability. People get a kick out of saying, "This is what I did, and I didn't have to try hard."

While in my undergrad history class, we were given a ten-page paper to write. We were given this assignment at the beginning of the semester, and it was due at the end of the semester. Unfortunately, I waited until the last minute and pulled an all-nighter to write this paper. I turned the paper in, and the next class period the professor told the class that he wanted to highlight a paper that was excellent. I was sure it wasn't my paper, but behold, he announced it was mine. He shared how it was evident that I had started the paper at the beginning of the semester because of how good it was. Outside I was smiling hard, but inside I was thinking, "If he only knew." After class I told some of my classmates what had happened, and I made it seem like I hadn't really tried that hard and still received an A! I was operating out of performance goals and not learning goals. When I look back, I think of how much better the paper could have been if I had spent more time on it. I cheated myself by not giving my all or my best. I did not have a learning mindset.

A learning mindset is about developing competency and growing, while performance orientation focuses on comparison with others (doing it for oneself versus competing with others). Performance-oriented people aren't necessarily concerned with mastery. They may not give their best as long as their results are better than other people's results. Most people tend to lean toward performance because that is how we have been conditioned. We are "performing" from birth as we are rated on our weight. When we are in school, we are rated and put in certain homerooms. We are then rated to perform for high school graduation rankings, then college graduation rankings, and it continues. There have even been companies that ranked their employees and terminated the lowest 10 percent. We have a performance-oriented society. Can you see how hard it can be to have a learning mindset? Too many people spend their energy trying to prove their worth and are losing out on time and effort in simply being their worth.

We are not 100 percent learning oriented or 100 percent performance oriented. Different moments in our lives and different situations bring out different orientations at times. To become more learning oriented, we have to stop asking, "Am I good?" and start asking, "Am I getting better?" Those who achieve more focus on the latter. When we are trying to get better, we generally spend more time learning and listening versus proving and showing.

When we focus on getting better, we find our work more enjoyable, interesting, and engaging. I like all three of those things, and I think work can be all of them!

People spend too much time trying to prove their worth, versus simply being their worth.

Growth Mindset versus Fixed Mindset

Growth mindset people believe their intelligence can be developed; thus, they outperform those who believe their intelligence is fixed (fixed mindset). A growth mindset is more than effort. You need three things: effort, new strategies, and seeking input from others. Carol Dweck states, "Individuals who believe their talents can be developed (through hard work, good strategies, and input from others) have a growth mindset. They tend to achieve more than those with a more fixed mindset (those who believe their talents are innate gifts). This is because they worry less about looking smart and they put more energy into learning."[9] Growth mindset is not simply being flexible, open-minded, or having a positive outlook. It involves the three areas above. To be clear, a pure growth mindset doesn't exist; it is not something that we are born with, nor do we have it all the time. Thus, it is important to intentionally focus on having more growth-mindset experiences and knowing our fixed-mindset triggers.

Some fixed-mindset triggers are being overly anxious or shying away from new and challenging things. When you face failure, do you feel defeated and incompetent? Does criticism bring out your fixed mindset, and do you become defensive, angry, or growth paralyzed instead of being interested in how you can learn from the feedback? What do you do when someone else does something better than you that you value? Do you feel threatened or envious, or does it spur you to learn?

> With a learning mindset you will engage your work
> with more effort and creativity.

When you operate with a learning mindset, it will help you to engage your work with more effort and creativity while minimizing harmful negative thoughts about yourself and your work. This mindset is critical for your long-term growth and development and ultimately will help you to achieve more when connected to your Why. While it is important to know this information for your Now, the bigger question is what will you do? Here are some practical tips to help you engage now!

Practical Tips

Tip 1: When working on a task or a project, focus more on the process that leads to learning (hard work or trying new things) than on the results. There was this amazing company that achieved great results, called Enron, but they are no longer a company, partly because they didn't focus on the process and this "little" thing called ethics. Focusing on the process helps to foster a growth mindset and the inherent benefits it provides.

Tip 2: Stretch yourself with training and development (in-house, external conference, web-based, continued education). There are many ways to grow and exercise that learning mindset.

Tip 3: Develop an achievement hobby. Individuals who have a hobby where they are able to achieve tend to have a spillover effect into their work lives. What is one area outside of work that you can begin to master (running, collecting, building furniture, a cause, bodybuilding, trekking/hiking, cycling, etc.)? These can help in driving your motivation and achievement behaviors.

Tip 4: Challenge your victimhood and cultivate more positive emotions. Many people who are performance oriented see themselves as the victim. Use the Three Lens Approach, where you challenge the stories you are telling yourself at work and home.

(1) Reverse Lens: What would the other person in this conflict say, and in what ways might that be true? (2) Long Lens: How will I most likely view this situation in six months? (3) Wide Lens: Regardless of the outcome of this issue, how can I grow and learn from it?[10]

These are practical ways to kick normal out the door and develop more of a learning mindset.

Whew! There was quite a bit to process in this chapter. You may want to identify a tip you deem as important and focus on it this week. Take your time to discover what will work best for you, because when you consistently embrace learning as a mindset, it will help you to give more effort and get more done. We shouldn't settle for normal, but we must keep learning, developing, and improving now!

KEY TAKEAWAYS AND TIPS

p When you are on cruise control, you move from a state of being active to a state of being passive. Things are happening around you and you may be coasting. One way to challenge your cruise control is by first acknowledging you have pressed it and by incorporating new tasks, challenges, and goals into what you are doing.

p Take the Birthday Challenge and do one thing by each birthday that you have never done and either have always wanted to do or that will challenge you (i.e., run a marathon, write a book, work on that exciting project, take that vacation, adopt a child, etc.).

p One way to be more mindful is to conduct a Plus/Delta with the most important people in your life and identify what you are doing well and what you can change/ improve on.

p When you have a learning mindset, it is about growing, learning from failure, and giving the best you can. When you have a performance mindset, it is about looking good, avoiding failure, and only giving what makes you look better than others.

p Stop asking, "Am I good?" and start asking, "Am I getting better?" Those who achieve more focus on the latter.

Chapter 9

PROGRESS:
The Principle of the Frog, Step, Seed, and Smile

David Gates: President of Atmos Energy/Former Chairman of Mississippi Chamber of Commerce

Sitting at his desk, David ponders the unique challenges facing him as the leader of his organization, and he is inspired by recalling how far he has come. David has always loved training. Actually, the training program was one of the things that intrigued him about his first company. However, David didn't need a formal training program to advance, grow, and learn because he treated his whole career, both good and bad, as his personal training program.

David's first assignment out of his company's official training program was into a job called "non-revenue engineering," which he deemed as pretty boring. He remembers thinking, "Man, if I'm

93

going to have to do this the rest of my career, this is not going to last long." While his work colleagues may have loved this work, David did not, but he knew he could learn something from the time and experience. He learned this progress principle on his first job out of college, where part of the learning experience was digging ditches. He recalls that time: "I'm wearing myself out. I'm thinking I'm pretty young. I'm in pretty good shape, and these older guys are leaving me in the dust. Taking the time to listen and learn and realize, even something as simple as digging a ditch, there's an art to it. There's a technique to it, and there's a professionalism to what they do every day. I can learn from that. Then, hopefully, I can learn and apply that to some of the other areas of my life." David is unique, as he learned early on that it wasn't about necessarily loving what he did that would help him achieve, but rather learning from what he did that would help him achieve. While others have complained, David has been intentionally progressing and achieving more.

Progress can be one of the biggest motivators for workers. Before I explain what progress is, it is important to explain what progress is not. It is not always clamoring for what you don't have. The kind of progress I am talking about is a mix between contentment and growth. To be content does not mean you have to be complacent, but it does mean you have an appreciation of your present space. Bigger, newer, and more aren't always better. The better is when you give your best where you are, with what you have!

A part of being "On 10" is making meaningful progress, and the principle covered in this chapter will help you do just that. I have found through research, interviews, and experience that there are four things that can help you better engage, perform, and ultimately achieve more progress. As we work through these four things, think of applying them on a daily or weekly basis. There are some people who can apply these four things in a daily rhythm based on their job and role, and others can apply them on a weekly rhythm. Identify what works best for you and start progressing now! These four items are what I call the Principle of the Frog, Step, Seed, and Smile.

Bigger, newer, and more aren't always better. Better is giving your best with what you have!

The key to implementing these into your life is planning. If you will do these four things daily, then you should plan the day before (a tomorrow list) or first thing in the morning what you will do and when you will do it. Don't create a to-do list, but schedule it in your calendar. You will accomplish more this way.

THE PRINCIPLE OF THE FROG, STEP, SEED, AND SMILE

My clients wanted a practical framework that could help their employees give more effort, be more productive, and feel better about their work. The Principle of the Frog, Step, Seed, and Smile was the answer to that request. This principle should be applied either daily or weekly, whichever makes the most sense for your schedule and rhythm of life. Each of the four items of this principle are based on research and common sense and can help you to make progress and engage your Now.

The Frog

Mark Twain is quoted as saying, "Eat a live frog first thing in the morning, and nothing worse will happen to you the rest of the day." Brian Tracy, the goal guru, wrote a book called *Eat That Frog*, inspired by Mark Twain's quote. The frog represents your most challenging task of the day. It encompasses something that is harder than everything else. What is your biggest work priority to accomplish that day or week? This is most likely your frog. You want to eat your frog early in the day or in the week. *Go hard early!*

What you do first thing in the morning/week should be something that is challenging and or daunting and takes a lot of focus and determination. This is important due to the law of diminishing returns and our limitations on self-control. The longer the day and week, the more fatigue sets in. The less energy, focus, and motivation we will have. The more likely we will push that challenging task off to the next day and the next day, until the frog becomes a dragon breathing fire down your back. Do your biggest and most challenging tasks first.

The first thing you do in the morning/week should be challenging and daunting.

I travel by airplane quite a bit. While researching and writing this book, I found that when I challenged myself to read at least one journal article before watching a movie or taking a nap, I accomplished more than reading that one article. If I said, "I am going to watch a movie first and then read an article," the latter rarely happened. Do the hardest task first!

Tip for the Frog: For your most difficult tasks, take uninterrupted time in the morning. If you work in an office where it's difficult to have uninterrupted time, come in earlier, when no one is there, and work on your frog of the day; then leave earlier. If you are unable to leave earlier, maybe you can take a longer lunch and work out during this break. Don't answer your email first thing and get caught in the email trap and its power to zap you of your super productivity powers. Once you have eaten that frog, your day might just feel lighter.

The Step

The step represents moving forward in an area or a task that is meaningful and significant to you, the individual. This is not progress for progress' sake, but this task or project excites you and energizes you. This is such a simple but hidden concept. In a study conducted with 669 managers from dozens of companies around the world, 95 percent of managers failed to identify the number-one managerial tool that affects employee motivations and emotions, which is progress. In their research of twenty-six project teams from seven companies, they found by reviewing nearly twelve thousand daily diary entries that the most common element that triggered a person's best day was progress in the work. Either one's own progress or the team's progress, even incremental progress. They found steps forward were a part of 76 percent of people's best mood days.[1] Do you see why this is important? When people are positive, they are more committed and care more for their colleagues. This inner work life can be somewhat of a fuel for work performance. While this study focused on correlations and not causation, the link between positivity and progress is unmistakable. The researchers noticed that the individuals were more intrinsically motivated, they were more positive toward challenges in their work, and they had a sense of accomplishment. The participants possessed more positive perceptions, happiness, and satisfaction, and were more engaged! Wow! They sound like . . . dah da da dah . . . *Super Employees* (movie rights pending)!

Tip for the Step: Make a list of seven goals (personal or professional) that you want to accomplish in the next ten years. If you could only achieve one of those goals, which one would have the biggest and best impact on your life? Now, how can you do something toward that goal every single day, even if it is incremental (inspired by Brian Tracy)? What is one thing that, if accomplished, could make you feel you had made meaningful progress—a small win? It could be the frog, but maybe not. Visualize and ask yourself this question the moment you begin your workday and workweek. The workday or workweek has been completed, and you feel you have had an amazing amount of achievement. What did you do to feel that way? Everyday progress and small wins can make all the difference in how people perform and feel internally.

The Seed

The seed represents learning and growth. It represents continually challenging oneself to develop and learn something new. This is important because when people are learning, they feel more and more competent and they are creating psychological resources. This points back to the learning mindset, which allows them to be open to more new ideas. This type of learning can be formal or informal. The learning might include continuous learning programs at work. It could be a podcast, an industry magazine or newsletter, a chapter of a book, a video, another person, or something else. This could be something as simple as fifteen minutes out of your day, or it could be more substantial, like a full-day training program. You have to find the right mix for yourself, but no matter what, do it consistently. Pretty soon you will see these seeds turn into giant trees of knowledge and practice as you embrace your Why and Now.

Tip for the Seed: Identify how you will learn daily or weekly. Be very intentional in planning this in your schedule. Share what you learn with someone else, as this increases the likelihood that you will remember it, understand it, and use it in the future.

The Smile

Awww, I am getting warm fuzzies already, but don't mistake the fuzzies for not being helpful. The smile is special because it's not about you smiling, but about bringing a smile to someone else's face. How can you make someone else feel appreciated and valued? When you bring a smile to someone else's face, it gives you great benefits and more positive associations and can lead to more energy and effort toward fulfilling your Why with passion. While you do not have to specifically select someone from work, you should try to include people in your workplace. Positive relationships at work energize people. Not only is friendship great at work, but also outside of work. Friendship outside of work hours is associated with higher levels of well-being, less disengagement, and higher task performance the following week at work. According to this research, I guess the TV show *Friends* was secretly about productivity at work!

> Bringing a smile to someone else's face benefits
> not only that person, but also you.

You should have daily or weekly IMOAs. No, this is not a combination of champagne and orange juice, and no, it does not have its origins on the islands of Hawaii. IMOAs are Intentional Moments of Appreciation. An IMOA is not a simple "thank you" or "good job." It is purposeful, specific, and thoughtful. IMOAs include, but aren't limited to, a handwritten thank-you note, thoughtful email, phone call, lunch meeting, or even a brief conversation. Have fun with it and realize that when we make others smile, it benefits us as well. Our well-being is improved and we have a more positive attitude. I once had a client who, during one of our meetings, mentioned that she was dog training. She was so nice to me that after our meeting, I sent her a little book on successfully training your dog. Even though I didn't see her smile when she received it, I envisioned her appreciating a small token of appreciation. I benefited internally from doing something thoughtful for her.

Tip for the Smile: Think about doing thirty days of IMOAs to jump-start your appreciation journey. Plan ten to fifteen minutes every day to intentionally appreciate someone. You could write thirty thank-you cards, make thirty IMOA calls, or send thirty IMOA emails. You know what's the best? When you get the person's voicemail and you leave an amazing message that they can save and listen to later when they are having a challenging day. Choose to invest in others' happiness for thirty consecutive days and see how you feel. I bet it will be amazing!

Reflecting, planning, and applying these four principles will lead to greater progress in your work and life. When you do the hardest thing first (frog), make a meaningful step forward (step), continue to actively learn and grow (seed), and intentionally appreciate others (smile), this will help you to feel better about your work, achieve greater satisfaction in your life, and appropriately deal with failure.

FAILURE AS FUEL

Anthony Gorrity: Entrepreneur, Professor, and Digital Media Specialist

On his typical way home from work, Anthony had some not-so-typical news to share with his wife. He wondered how he could have let this happen, and he didn't know how he would share this horrible news. How would she react? Would she still trust in him? How would they survive this? They had just gotten married, and through the marriage Anthony had become a dad. They had just obtained their slice of the "American dream" by purchasing their first home. Anthony needed to tell her, but he wondered how. He mustered up enough strength to tell her that he had just been laid off from his position at one of the oil and gas companies in Houston, Texas. What came next shouldn't have been a surprise for Anthony, as his wife motivated him and encouraged him to try something new based on what he loved to do. She said to him, "You've always been creative; you like to draw. You like to make things. Why don't we go to the art institute and check out some of the programs there and see if there's something creative that you can do?" They went to a computer lab at the art institute, and he was fascinated by the creative work the students produced. He thought to himself, "I can do that!" While he didn't end up at the art institute, he attended another institution and now teaches alongside the professors who taught him.

Great feel-good story, right? Not so fast, as Anthony recalled feeling like he had been robbed when he was laid off from the oil and gas company. One day he had a job, and the next day he didn't. While he wasn't laid off because of poor performance, it still hurt that he was the "fat" that was trimmed. Anthony states, "I just remember, it was kind of depressing at first, but then once I finally started to begin on the path of living out my Why, the depression or sadness started to become happiness, and it all worked out in the end." Anthony didn't allow this failure to be final but rather used it as fuel for his Why and ultimately his life. Fortunately, he had his amazing wife to inspire him. Now, doesn't that feel good!

I like to say, "If at some point you aren't failing, you aren't trying hard enough!" How do you handle failure? Does it crush you, or does it challenge you to learn a new way or figure out a new path? I also love the saying, "Failure is not final, unless you allow it to be." Did you know that J. K. Rowling (the author of the widely unheard-of Harry Potter book series) was a single mom on welfare when she started writing *Harry Potter*? Did you also know that Oprah was fired from her first television job as a Baltimore TV anchor? There are so many examples of people who have failed and allowed it to fuel them. Think of all the inventions and innovation that have come from failure. At the same time, there are numerous examples of people who failed, gave up, and ceased to try anything new. They allowed failure to be final.

If at some point you aren't failing, you aren't trying hard enough!

I remember when I first started my speaking business. I had just been honored by *Ebony* magazine as one of their "30 Young Leaders on the Rise." I had also been selected by my graduate school, where I was pursuing my MBA, as the Student Entrepreneur of the Year. I went to the leadership office at the school and asked them if I could speak to the new students. I even used the three magic words: *at a discount*. You know what they told me? No! I was crushed. I felt that if they did not believe in me, who would believe in me? I was genuinely hurt. I contemplated giving up the business. At that moment, I decided that I could either cry about it or do something about it. So I cried a little; then I humbled myself and scheduled a meeting with them. I wanted to know why they'd said no so I could eventually get them to say yes. They shared that they mainly hired people from certain agencies and conferences. I took copious notes. I later became a member of one of those agencies and started speaking at some of those conferences, and guess what eventually happened? Years later, they brought me back to speak—for full price! One of the people who had told me no even went to work for another school and had me speak to her students. I turned that failure into fuel for where I am now, where I am consulting and speaking fifty to sixty times a year to professionals, organizations, associations, and educational institutions. I could have given up that day.

What about you? Can you recall a time when you were about to give up and you didn't? What do you want to give up on now that you can possibly use as fuel for your progress?

Martin Seligman, considered the father of positive psychology, did a study in 1960 and discovered learned helplessness (where a person suffers from a sense of powerlessness or a constant inability to succeed). The study showed that human beings who experienced a loud noise and could not control it would eventually just accept it without even trying to escape. There were three groups. The first group heard a noise and could push a button to stop it. The second group could not turn off the noise, even by trying hard to turn it off. The third group could hear no noise. Later, each of the groups were faced with a new situation involving noise. All they had to do was move their hands twelve inches to turn it off. The first and third groups realized this and turned it off. Those in the second group generally did nothing. Because they had "learned" in phase 1 of the research that they could do nothing, they later became passive (learned helplessness). The group expected more failure and didn't even try to end the noise. However, Seligman also discovered that even in the face of failure and inescapable noise, about a third of the participants never became helpless. He called this "real optimism."[2] Real optimists see setbacks and failure as temporary and changeable, and they believe they can do something about it. Are you a real optimist?

> In order to engage our Now, we must see failure
> properly—as fuel!

Remember what Nietzsche shared and Kanye reminded us: "That which does not kill us makes us stronger!" It is so easy to hear or see someone say, "Learn from failure," but only you can choose to reframe failure not as a negative but as a learning experience to move forward. If you can see failure as fuel, it will help you to continue in passionate pursuit of your Why and to do it Now. Too many people (myself included) have allowed failure to decrease their effort as they licked their wounds. In order to engage our Now, we must see failure properly—as fuel!

KEY TAKEAWAYS AND TIPS

p How do you evaluate yourself and assess your progress? Sports players watch film. What is your film-watching process? Who are the key stakeholders in your life that you can get real and honest feedback from so that you can progress?

p The frog is the most challenging thing that you have to accomplish in a day or week. The step is doing something, even incrementally, that has great meaning for you. The seed is engaging in a learning activity that will help you grow and think more creatively about what you do. The smile is engaging in an IMOA (Intentional Moment of Appreciation) where you encourage and appreciate others. When you apply the Principle of the Frog, Step, Seed, and Smile, it can help you to have more progress, be more productive, and even have more energy/effort for your given tasks.

p Stop making to-do lists and start putting your to-dos into your actual schedule. It will be less frustrating, and if you stick to it, you will accomplish more.

p Remember: If at some point you aren't failing, then you aren't trying hard enough!

p If you struggle with being a real optimist or finding positive things in general, try this exercise: before bed each night, write down three things from the day that you are thankful for. This will help you rewrite and reframe experiences in a positive light.

You are on a roll. You just completed part 2 and have seen the importance of your Now and how being passionate and "On 10" can serve you well to accomplish more goals, give more effort, and be more productive. The crux of this book is the intersection of the Why and the Now concepts in part 3. As you jump in, remember that you need both to truly achieve more.

Part Three

Your WHY Matters NOW:
Practical Action Steps

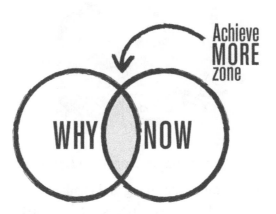

*It is never too late to be
what you might have been.*

—George Eliot

Chapter 10

PURSUE:
The Why Matters Now
Quadrants

Katie Eubanks: Features Editor for a Large Metro Paper

Finishing a pretty time-consuming and challenging week pushed Katie to reflect on her "busy" life. Katie is an extremely hard-working millennial. She writes weekly columns, proofreads people's work, oversees stories/photos/videos, promotes those stories/photos/videos, helps grow the digital aspect of the paper, oversees big projects, hangs out with friends, participates at church, and did I mention she finds time to breathe? Katie states, "I probably fall more on the work, work, work side, sort of for-getting about the big picture. I sometimes associate activity with progress and getting things done." If you are like Katie, please raise your hand (author of this book awkwardly and slowly raises hand). It's not so hard to see why Katie says she often finds herself in the Misplaced quadrant (more on that in a minute). What amazes me with Katie is that she takes the time to reflect and learn how she can improve. What about you? Which quadrant do you fall into, and how can you improve?

This chapter will help you better understand where you might lean regarding the Why and the Now. I have found that people generally either have a high Why and a low Now, or they have a low Why and a high Now. This chapter will not only help those two types of people, but also give practical advice on what to do even if you have a low Why and a low Now. Get ready to engage both in the following sections and not only achieve, but achieve more.

THE FOUR TYPES

Pop quiz! Do you remember the three types of people as it relates to achievement? Here is a cheat sheet. There are those who do not achieve, those who achieve, and those who achieve more. This translates to the Why/Now Venn diagram you have seen. Figure A is what it looks like for those who do not achieve. Figures B and C are what it looks like for those who achieve. Figure D is what it looks like for those who achieve more. The "more" is brought forward because of this powerful intersection in what we called earlier the Achieve More Zone (AMZ). Remember: this "more" is an internal comparison, not an external one.

Figure A "Do Not Achieve"	Figure B "Achieve"	Figure C "Achieve"	Figure D "Achieve MORE"

What's your type? No, I am not trying to offer you a pickup line. In my research, I have noticed that there are generally four different types of people as it relates to this combination of Why and Now. It's important to know your type because it allows you to know how to specifically and intentionally combine your Why and your Now and achieve more. As you can see in the Why Matters Now Quadrant, the four types are as follows:

- Low Why, Low Now: The Wanderer
- High Why, Low Now: The Thinker
- Low Why, High Now: The Misplaced
- High Why, High Now: The Pursuer

Let's discuss each type, what happens if you stay in each quadrant too long, and what each type looks like as a leader, and I'll give you some general tips for each type on how to gain a greater balance of your Why and Now.

Knowing your type allows you to combine your Why and Now to achieve more.

The Wanderer

This type of person does not know their Why, or their Why is unclear. Wanderers don't understand purpose, and to some degree they are just existing. Not only do they not know their Why, but they generally aren't living their life with any level of passion. If I had to give them a TV show, I would jokingly call them *The*

Walking Dead, because they are not activated by a Why and are not doing anything about it Now. They may be passive and haven't activated their courage to act. This type generally does not achieve. I spoke at one educational institution and conducted a workshop on the Your Why Matters Now concept. As people shared their Macro Why Statements (MaWS), one specific student said he didn't make a difference and that he spent 99 percent of his time in his room. It was clear to me that he did not know his Why, nor the power of his Now.

If in this quadrant too long: They can feel down on themselves and feel a sense of despair as if they are wasting their life away. There is a high possibility that they live with regrets. They can sometimes believe that this is how life will always be for them.

As leaders: Wanderers generally won't step up to lead. They will shy away from opportunities to take initiative.

Tips for the Wanderer: See the value that a life truly lived can have!

- Strength: They can start with a clean slate. They haven't adopted the negative behaviors of the other styles, so when they activate their Why, they won't have to overcome patterns of negative behavior in either the Why or the Now.
- The Wanderer needs to first spend some time in reflection identifying his or her Why. Chapter 4 ("Discover: What Is Your True Why?") would be a great chapter to master, as uncovering one's Why is vital.

- Wanderers desperately need a mentor and/or coach who will help guide them and encourage them toward the right direction. They can also use an accountability partner who will walk with them and challenge them to pursue greater levels of achievement.
- Wanderers should ask themselves the Four Questions: Where am I now? Where do I want to be? What are the barriers preventing me from getting there? How can I remove those barriers? These questions answered honestly can help assess where they are and how to get where they want to be.
- In certain situations, this type of person should see a counselor to help process his or her emotional and mental state. With an extreme emotional state, the disconnect may be deeper than simply discovering the person's Why and unleashing his or her Now.

The Thinker

The Thinker knows their Why, they understand purpose, and they comprehend their motivations and intent, but for whatever reason they aren't giving maximal effort. This group can be characterized as dreamers, or people who take little to no action. Some of the reasons this person may not act are fear of failure, fear of success, or trying to please family, colleagues, or friends. Thinkers are known to procrastinate.

In *The Now Habit*, Neil Fiore talks about procrastination not as a problem, but as a symptom. Procrastination is not the issue, he says, but rather it is the unfolding of a real issue. One of the ideas he presents is that maybe people are afraid to be judged on their best, so instead of giving their all, they wait and try with limited time. This is a defense mechanism, just in case whatever they are working on is not successful. Unfortunately, this thinking can minimize the potential impact of their efforts.[1]

This group achieves, but generally does not "achieve more." For example: After an event at a financial institution, a woman came up to me and shared that for the last ten years she had thought of writing a book. She knew it would help people, but she always made excuses why she couldn't or why people would not read it. I shared the mantra for this quadrant, which is, "A dream that is never acted upon is really a nightmare in disguise!" My friends, it is time to wake up from the nightmare and act.

HIGH **WHY**

THE THINKER

LOW **NOW** ◄——————► HIGH **NOW**

LOW **WHY**

If in this quadrant too long: The longer they stay in this quadrant, the harder it will potentially be to act. They can turn inward and be overly sensitive of criticism that challenges their plan or their perceived high-achiever status.

As leaders: When they lead, they usually lead with their thoughts and best-laid plans and not necessarily their action. They are more comfortable telling people what to do than showing people what to do.

Tips for the Thinker: Stop waiting for the eighth day of the week!

- Strength: Many Thinkers are notorious for getting things right, and one aspect of their perfectionist tendencies is that they are helpful in processing plans thoroughly.
- The Thinker needs to be challenged to act and act with conviction and passion, as Thinkers struggle with analysis paralysis. Sometimes the hardest thing for people to do is to just start. One of my sayings is "Start big by

starting small; at least just start!" A Thinker should identify that one thing he or she can do to get the momentum going.

- Thinkers need to move from being perfectionists to being progressionists. They need to constantly remind themselves that it's okay to make mistakes—smart mistakes, but mistakes nonetheless.

- Seek advice and feedback from people who were in a similar situation. Having helpful data points from informed people will help Thinkers feel it's okay to act and move forward without 100 percent of the information.

- This person could also benefit from a PrAP (Professional Accountability Partner) with whom they meet regularly to talk about their goals and what they are going to do. When the PrAPs meet the next week or month, they will have either accomplished their goal or have to answer why they didn't do it. It's like having a partner to go to the gym even when you don't want to go. This will help move the Thinker to thoughtful action.

- Some of my research revealed that people who are used to being high achievers can fall into this category because they want to avoid situations or challenges that can tarnish their brand as a high achiever.

- Thinkers could benefit from placing themselves in situations and experiences where they are uncomfortable and do not know a lot (i.e., the Birthday Challenge). This will help them learn to act without all the data. Colin Powell was known to share that he acted on 75 percent of information because when perfect came, it would be too late.

The Misplaced

This is the quadrant where our friend Katie fell. The Misplaced are great at action. They are known for being active; however, these people may be active in the wrong places. They are impulsive and make bad or rushed decisions. They are likely to confuse activity with progress. They feel they are okay as long as they have filled up their schedule with things to do, places to go, and boxes to check off. They aren't often being guided by their Why, purpose, or intent but rather by whether they are busy or not.

My family used to live in Baltimore, Maryland, and I commuted to take graduate classes in the Washington, DC, area. One day I was running late, and we were speeding through the streets of Baltimore to get to the train station. I remember catching my breath, jumping out of the car, and running with everything I had to make the train. I was running so fast, people may have confused me with Usain Bolt for a brief moment. I remember running down the stairs and jumping with exuberance onto the train as the doors closed behind me. It felt like a movie scene. I even wiped the sweat from my brow. The conductor briskly walked through the train shouting two things, "All aboard" and "Tickets, please." Uh-oh! I didn't know where my ticket was. I wondered if I'd left it in the car or at home. I checked my pockets and breathed a sigh of relief. I found my ticket. I proceeded to give my ticket to the conductor. He took my ticket, looked at me, and said, "Sir, this train is going to Delaware." Small geography lesson. Delaware is north of Baltimore and Washington, DC, is south of Baltimore. I began to argue with the conductor and said emphatically, "Sir, I am going to DC." He said to me with a calm yet stern, straight face, "Sir, in forty-five minutes you will see exactly where you are going." I began to look out the windows and noticed this was not the normal way to DC. It then hit me. I was running so fast through the train station that I didn't even check to make sure I got on the right train. I arrived to class very late that day because of a personal "detour."

Moral of the story: When you are misplaced, you might be running through life so fast that you aren't checking to make sure you are getting on your Why train, and you may end up at your destination later than you wanted, if you make it at all.

If in this quadrant too long: The Misplaced can believe that they are successful based on what they do and not on who they are. They may begin to engage in unhealthy behaviors because they are not resting and reflecting.

As leaders: When they lead, they can sometimes confuse moving their employees (getting them to do something) with motivating their employees (getting them to want to do something). They consistently change plans based on the whims of the moment.

Tips for the Misplaced: Get on the right train!

- Strength: Getting things done. They are prone to action and are risk takers. They are willing to try new things and embrace the learning curve of innovation.
- One way to assess if they are on the right train is to first identify what their Why is and if their current train is leading them to that destination. If not, they may consider getting off at the next stop and getting on the train that is headed to their Why destination. The closest people in their life can also help them assess if they are on the right train. Be careful, because this Misplaced type often confuses doing good things with doing great things, and it can be challenging for them to let things go, because they do not want to feel as if they are losing out.
- One tool to help them is planning out their time. Because they operate from a doing mentality and can

be impulsive, it is best for the Misplaced to schedule their time in advance of the week and the day in order to better align their actions with their Why.

- This type needs consistent and scheduled intentional moments of reflection to make sure that they are headed in the right direction. Whether monthly or quarterly, they need to conduct their own internal Plus/Delta.
- They need consistent reminders of their Why. They need to engage with people they trust to consistently remind them of their Why. They could benefit from keeping images, pictures, and objects around that remind them of their Why.
- They need to create a "good" and "great" list and identify the good, helpful things they are doing and the great things they could be doing that are more in line with their Why. Once they have identified the good things, they need to determine what they can stop doing altogether or momentarily. This type has to learn how to let go of the good in order to make room for the great.

The Pursuer

The mighty Pursuers. This group clearly knows their purpose and Why. They keep it before them consistently, and they are strongly connected to it. You could encounter them out in public and ask them their Macro Why Statement, and they would be able to share it with you easily. This group is "On 10" and giving their all. They realize that this moment matters, and they try to live a life with no regrets. This is their aim. This is their goal. One does not always reside in this quadrant, but one can increase time spent in this quadrant.

Jordan Rice and I met in college and remain close to this day. We have done many things in our journey (including jumping out of a plane together), and while imperfect, Jordan spends much of his time in this quadrant. Jordan remembers being in law school and going out that first night with other students. These law students were talking about law nonstop, and Jordan wasn't all that interested in talking about it unless it was on the test. He states, "They really had a burden for it, a real passion, and it was through seeing other people's passion for things that I actually got jealous in a good way. I realized that I wanted to do something that I was really 'hot' about." While Jordan would go on to become a successful family court attorney and child advocate lawyer, he still felt that he hadn't found that special something. Jordan would later find that the special something burning inside of him was becoming a pastor of a multiethnic church. When Jordan caught the vision, he began to act. He went to seminary, interned at a multiethnic church, worked with a chaplain at Sing Sing prison, and eventually moved to Harlem, where he is now the founding pastor of Renaissance Church NYC, a growing multiethnic church that brings together people like investment bankers and teenagers from the hood to serve a common purpose. While discovering his Why, Jordan did not stop being a lawyer, but he tried some things out. His advice to us is, "Shoot bullets, not cannonballs." He describes that as testing things out in small ways, not making drastic changes right away. While others may have simply dreamed about pursuing their Why, Jordan woke up and put his Why into action. We have a lot to learn from amazing people like Jordan.

If in this quadrant too long: Great! Stay as long as you can, because this is where you don't merely achieve but you achieve more. *As leaders:* Pursuers not only know their Why but they inspire the Why in the individuals on their team. They are motivators and encourage people to take strategic risks and to stretch themselves. They generally operate with a learning mindset.

Tips for the Pursuer: Keep going!

- Strength: They achieve more, as they are strongly connected to their Why and they pursue it with passion. They are generally knowledgeable about what they commit to and seek to master their areas of focus.

- This is a quadrant where people strive to be, and when challenges or difficulties arise, they can sometimes resort back to either the Thinker or the Misplaced.

- Mentoring others helps this group stay focused, but it is also critical for them to have a mentor to challenge them to continue achieving more.

- It is important for them to continue challenging themselves and taking on stretch assignments. Without consistent challenges, they may become bored and start coasting or pressing cruise control.

- Stay humble! Sometimes Pursuers can have little patience and tolerance for those who are not. They may desire for everyone to be pursuing like them, but they must realize everyone has their own journey.

Are you thinking, "Well, what if I am all four?" What I have found is that you can be Misplaced in one area of your life and a Pursuer in another. Generally, you tend to reside in one quadrant more than others, but it is possible to be in multiple quadrants in the different areas of your life. If this is you, so that you are not overwhelmed, work on one quadrant area that you might want to improve. If you see yourself as being in one quadrant in particular, utilize the tips to move forward in achieving more. The Why Matters Now Quadrant was designed to be self-reflective to help you process the areas of your life according to your Why and Now. It is not meant to be scientifically proven, but is a helpful tool for processing your journey. If you struggle with identifying your main quadrant, then share this section with three to five of your closest friends and ask them what fits you the most.

THE DARK SIDE OF OVERACHIEVERS

I feel the need to address an important issue, and that is of the overachievers. Depending on who you ask, being an overachiever can be a positive or a negative. However, overachievers are not to be confused with those who achieve more. Those who achieve more are in the Achieve More Zone (AMZ) of the Why/Now Venn. Overachievers, as I define them, still only achieve because their focus is on short-term gains. People who overachieve are typically in the Misplaced quadrant, and sometimes they can be confused with Pursuers. Remember: Pursuers are guided by their Why and their Now. In the Jordan example above, if he had continued his journey toward being a successful lawyer (not a bad thing at all), people on the outside would have perceived him as a Pursuer, but he was not being guided by his Why. An extreme example of an overachiever is Jeffrey Skilling of Enron. It appeared that he was achieving, but in the long run he wasn't.

David McClelland, a late Harvard psychologist, spent years studying achievement and saw the downside of overachievers in that they tend to cut corners, cheat, and go at it alone. They are unhealthier in competition and aren't effective collaborators. The dark side of overachievers can be that they are performance oriented, ignore positive feedback, and obsess over criticism. Overachievers may command and coerce versus coach and collaborate. They motivate by results, regardless of how they are achieved.[2]

If you are an overachiever, spend time in reflection and identify a clear Why that intrinsically motivates you. Knowing if you are being guided by your Why is crucial because it can dictate your long-term authentic success moving ahead. You can do a lot of things, do a lot of those things with excellence, and people can think you are really achieving, but if you are not being guided by your Why, you are still Misplaced.

The dark side of overachievers is that they overly obsess with criticism and feedback.

Kathrine Switzer: First Woman to Officially Run the Boston Marathon

Another person who combined her Why and her Now was Kathrine Switzer. The day was April 19, 1967, and it was a cold and snowy day. This day was a special one as Kathrine Switzer lined up to be the first woman to officially run the Boston Marathon. Before entering she had been told that women couldn't run a marathon and that they did not have the strength to complete it. Kathrine was determined to show the world that a woman could in fact run and complete a marathon. She and a few male runners entered their team in the Boston Marathon. As race officials were handing out bibs, they gave her a race bib with the number 261. Soon after, the race began and they were off.

At close to mile 4 of this 26.2-mile journey, she noticed a figure with a dark coat standing in the middle of the road, trying to get her attention. She ran past him. A few moments later, she heard the unusually loud noise of someone running behind her, and as she abruptly turned to see who it was, the same man was now trying to violently tear off her bib number. This man was Jock Semple, the race manager, and he was trying to get this woman out of "his" race. While she continued to run, she processed the thoughts of amazement, embarrassment, and humiliation. She wanted to give up, but she quickly thought about the power of the moment and how much it could do for women in running, women in sports, and women in general. She not only continued to run, but she completed the race with blood-soaked socks at a time of four hours and twenty minutes. She pursued what many believed was impossible but what she knew all along was possible.

Kathrine Switzer went on to run many more marathons and founded the organization 261 Fearless Inc. in commemoration of her bib number that was almost pulled off. It is obvious that both her Why and her Now were high, and she has mentored many to continue pursuing, even in the face of adversity.

No matter what type you are, there is always room for learning and growth. The first step to moving forward is to know where you currently are. If you have been honest with yourself, then you can identify opportunities for growth and practical things that you can do starting today to begin to move toward the Pursuer quadrant more often.

KEY TAKEAWAYS AND TIPS

p Wanderers (Low Why, Low Now) don't know why they are doing something and aren't doing it with any level of great effort or passion. They need to first connect to a strong Why.

p Thinkers (High Why, Low Now) know why they are doing something and are strongly connected to purpose, but for whatever reason they aren't giving great effort or intensity. Thinkers make great decisions, but many times may fail to act. They need accountability.

p The Misplaced (Low Why, High Now) aren't sure why they are doing something, but they just want to do something. They may be impulsive, make bad decisions, and confuse activity with progress. They need intentional times for reflection.

p Pursuers (High Why, High Now) know why they are doing something and they are doing it with passion. They need great humility and a heart to help others. If they are not careful, they can regress; therefore, they need to consistently challenge themselves by learning, growing, and taking on new meaningful tasks.

Chapter 11

CHANGE:
It's Not as Easy *or*
as Hard as You Think

Kelly Jennings: NFL Player Turned Financial Counselor/Advisor

One day during a tough season, Kelly Jennings felt that he wasn't living his Why. Kelly played football, and not the front-yard-with-the-raked-leaves-during-Thanksgiving kind of football. He played the first-round-draft-pick, playing-for-the-Seattle-Seahawks-and-Cincinnati-Bengals-for-six-years type of football. He was living the dream of many people, but he knew this was not it for him. This shift had the potential to be a challenging change. In that moment Kelly wondered, "Who am I? What do I want to do?" He says, "The thing that kept coming up through my life, even where I was, was that I love people. I love helping people. I love sitting with people, and that sparked my mind on counseling." Kelly boldly left the NFL and went to a seminary to receive a master's degree in marriage and family therapy. This degree partnered with his finance degree from the University of Miami led him to help people as a financial advisor.

In sharing about the change, Kelly states, "It was harder than what I thought . . . I looked at football that I've done all my life, like twenty-some years, and I really searched myself and prayed, and really just realized that I still loved that game. Still love it, but my passion, that passion that I had was not there. And trying to figure out why? Why is it not there? Well, what is the passion that *is* there? It's people. Helping people. That thing kept coming up. But I didn't know how to help people . . . so I dove into counseling." Kelly went through a lot of changes, even physical and psychological changes, as he was using his brain in ways he hadn't used it in years. In processing the change, he says, "I knew [football] inside and out. You ask me anything, and I could tell you about the intricacies of the game. Counseling—I didn't know anything. So, it was a complete learning curve. Paradigm shift. I think that's what made it the hardest—the whole learning curve." Despite the challenges and daunting changes he faced, Kelly was ready to tackle every single one of them because his Why was that valuable and important.

Yep, it's that awesome word that everyone loves to hate. What do people say again? The only thing that is constant is what? Change! People loathe to hear they have to change something. I have generally seen two types of people when it comes to change: those who are super cocky and don't think it will be that hard, and those who are super timid and think it will be way too hard. Be in the middle. Let me share a story I once heard about a captain and his ship.

Change happens, but what we do with that change
is vital.

In the 1400s there was a captain and his ship, and he saw three huge pirate ships coming to attack his ship. He immediately yelled to his first mate, "First mate, go grab me my sword and my red shirt!" His first mate grabbed both and gave them to him. The captain then feverishly put on his red shirt and began passionately fighting the pirates with his sword. He fought and fought until all the pirates and pirate ships began to retreat. That night at supper, his crew was rowdy and excited and yelled out to the captain, "Captain, we understand why you asked for the sword, but why did you ask for the red shirt?" The captain said, "Because if I would have been stabbed and begun to bleed, you never would have known, and you never would have lost momentum." His crew replied, "Wow, Captain! You are supersmart!"

The next day, ten pirate ships were on the horizon and getting ready to board the ship, and the captain yelled to his first mate, "First mate, grab me my sword . . . and my brown pants!" Ha! I promise you, you will get that one later if you don't get it now. The moral of the story is: *Change happens, but what we do with that change is vital.*

In order to achieve more, we must realize that proactive change is necessary. We must challenge the herd of society and embrace the discomfort that comes with doing something we've never done. This type of change requires the right kind of attitude in order to activate action in both the Why and the Now.

CHALLENGING THE HERD

Have you ever seen a group of people running and not known why they were running? You probably started running, too, didn't you? During my presentations, I do an experiential exercise. It's really a sight to see, especially if many people are in the location. I have my participants walk around their section of chairs or tables as fast as they can. Inevitably what happens is that anywhere from 75 percent to sometimes 100 percent of the people are all going the same way. This proves the real-life herd theory, from the article

"Geometry for the Selfish Herd" by biologist W. D. Hamilton.[1] Friedrich Nietzsche was also instrumental in describing the "herd instinct" in human society. Hamilton focused on a group of animals. When these animals thought danger was coming, they all began going the same way, even if that way was off a cliff. The question for us is, Where is our herd leading us? How is the herd in our life impacting our decisions to engage the Why and unleash the Now? The even bigger question is, Are you willing to take the uncomfortable position of challenging the herd? In a group of complaining people, will you start complaining too or share the positive you see? In a group of workers that are complaining about the manager and because of said manager they start working super slow, will you realize that your Why and Now matter to you no matter who is leading you? If you ever want to challenge the herd physically, walk on the left side of a busy sidewalk (especially in Manhattan) or in the mall. People will look at you funny . . . I get it all the time! In order to change, you have to be willing to challenge the herd. What herd do you need to challenge today? Sometimes the most challenging herd to go against are those who are closest to us. It can get uber uncomfortable.

Sometimes the most challenging herd to go against are those who are closest to us.

EMBRACING DISCOMFORT

Are you a hugger? When you see someone, do you walk to him or her with arms outstretched, or when people come to hug you, do you politely say to them, "Please do not touch me!"? Have you noticed that there are different types of hugs and greetings that exist? There is the formal greeting: the handshake. There is the "I'm cool" greeting—what is called the "dap" or the "bro hug." There is also the classic side hug. There is the I'm-going-to-hug-you-but-my-body-is-not-going-to-touch-you hug. Then there is the full frontal, where you squeeze the person as tight as you possibly can. I hope you don't run around your office or city giving full-frontal hugs, or security might be called. For many, the full-frontal hug is way too intimate and too close. Imagine I asked you to hug the closest person next to you for ninety seconds. I am not talking about that cute side hug, but rather that full frontal, I-am-going-to-squeeze-you-like-you-are-the-cushion-of-my-dreams type of hug. Most of us would be uncomfortable because that's too close. Even if we love to hug, we are not used to that type of hug for very long!

It's time for us to embrace that discomfort. No, I am not saying go to your next office meeting with arms outstretched, or you may no longer have office meetings to attend. But will you embrace your discomfort to go from 6 to being "On 10"? It takes a level of discomfort to do something challenging or that you have never done. Being uncomfortable is a sign of progress and should challenge you to focus more, not run and hide or procrastinate. As you begin to achieve more, I want to prepare you for the discomfort, because you will feel it, and I encourage you to try to embrace it.

Misery loves company, but average does too!

One area where you may feel this discomfort is in your circle. The people you allow to be closest to you. If you have been close with a bunch of people living on 6 and you challenge yourself to be "On 10," how do you think the sixes will respond? They might say, "We don't do 10 here; this is 6 land." I have learned something over the years, and I am sure you have too. *Misery loves company, but average does too!* If people are sixes, they may not want you to be "On 10" because that means that they might have to change and work differently, or be healthy, or challenge the boundaries of what they believe is possible. Is your Why important enough to you to get a little uncomfortable? If not, please go back to chapter

4 ("Discover: What Is Your True Why?"). But always remember: do not settle!

ATTITUDE ALTERATIONS

Dr. Kortni Alston: Happiness Scholar

Kortni was twenty-five years old and worked in the number-four market in the country as a television reporter. She was working her dream job and married to an amazing individual she calls her "soulmate." They were college sweethearts and were together for seven years. They had been married for only two months when the unthinkable occurred. Her husband was fatally shot. This accidental shooting made headlines, and Kortni was beyond devastated. She was hurt even more because that morning she had left early and regrettably didn't say goodbye to her husband. She thought to herself, "I'll speak to him later!" At the station, she got caught up in the news stories and never contacted him. She later found out that he had tragically lost his life. At the time of his death, she was helping her mother get through her first chemo treatment, as she had been diagnosed with cancer three weeks before Kortni's wedding. At one time, she was planning a funeral and helping her mother through the fight of her life. If anyone had a reason to be negative, it was Kortni. She surely grieved, but she used those moments to inspire her to truly value time. One way that she reminds herself of this is by wearing her former husband's watch for the last seventeen years as a constant reminder to value both her time and her Why.

Have you ever met someone who was always negative? They didn't have the Kortni reasons for being negative, but were just negative for what appeared to be no reason! You could say, "It sure is a beautiful day outside today," and they'd say, "But the sun is going down in five hours!" You could say, "We finished the project under budget!" and they'd say, "But you were over budget last time!" You could say, "I am finally taking my dream vacation," and they'd say, "They are probably going to have a hurricane, tornado, and earthquake all right before you leave!" Whoa! That's negative.

The Fill-the-Cup Mindset

Have you ever done the glass half-full/half-empty test as an assessment of your attitude? Well, let's do it right now. If you saw a glass that was half whatever, would you see that glass half-full or half-empty, or not even care?

I remember seeing a motivational speaker once who said, "If you can just see the glass as half-full, your life will be changed, everything will be different, and things will be amazing!" I thought to myself, "That's a bunch of crap." Some years after that, I was going through one of the toughest times in my life, a quarter-life crisis. I was lying in bed and remembered what he said, and I was honestly willing to try anything. I looked at a glass of water on the bedside table. I emphatically said to myself while lying in my messy bed, "Glass half-full, glass half-full!" I kept saying this until an idea crashed into my brain. It said, "Justin, why are you asking if this glass is half-empty or half-full when you can fill the stupid glass back up?" I finally got it.

Asking that question is a state of inaction. It takes action to fill the glass back up. I am not asking you to pour just anywhere, but into your glass. Pour into your Why, pour into you, and please pour now! What does your cup need to be filled with? Maybe a little Why, maybe a little Now, maybe a little of both.

One person who had the fill-the-cup mindset was Danielle Rice. Danielle was married to my friend Jordan, the one who went from lawyer to pastor of a multiethnic church.

On May 25, 2010, I spent my birthday with my family and a few friends, including Jordan and Danielle. We had a great time indoor rock climbing. Two weeks later I received a phone call from Jordan, and he was crying like I had never heard him do before. Through his tears I heard him say, "Justin, Danielle's been diagnosed with cancer." I sank into my seat at the train station in disbelief. Jordan said a tumor that they had found was cancerous and that Danielle had a rare form of cancer called cardiac angiosarcoma. She would likely only live for four months. I couldn't believe it. We had just been climbing together two weeks earlier.

When they went into the hospital room to share the news with Danielle, do you know what her first response was? She was obviously choked up a little bit, but she said, "Well . . . I guess it's a win-win situation. Either I will be healed, or I will be in heaven." When I heard this, I couldn't completely comprehend how a person on her death bed could see a win-win situation. Later I asked myself, "What's my problem?" How could I not see life as a win-win situation, no matter what is thrown at me or what I pick up along the way? I walked away from that experience with a mantra I try my hardest to live by every day, which is, "There are people who would love to have my days!" Danielle filled her cup, Jordan's cup, my cup, and the cups of all those who know her story with an overflow of amazing perspective! This has forever given me great perspective on my own attitude, especially when I start veering toward "woe is me" and feeling sorry for myself. After all, life isn't a road without twists, turns, and potholes.

Resilience will increase our odds of achieving more.

Resiliency

You are going to face bumps in the road, but will you continue? You are going to be stretched, but will you continue? You are going to work on some internal muscles you didn't know you had, and they may be sore some days, but will you continue? You will hear the *Frozen* anthem song another time, but will you continue? (I have little kids.) Are you resilient enough to continue? Resilience is "the capacity to rebound or bounce back from adversity, conflict, failure, or even positive events, progress, and increased responsibility." A positive mindset (confidence, optimism, and hope) develops resiliency.[2]

Ultimately, what we think about a task or goal is important. If we have an attitude of resilience, we will likely increase our effort and successfully increase our chances of achievement. The opposite is also true. What did Wayne Gretzky say? "You miss 100 percent of the shots you never take!" It's time to try. You don't have to wait for another moment to engage your Why and unleash your Now! Let me give you a tool that you can use to help you as you begin to navigate some of these changes. It's a tool I use in consulting and my personal life, called ADKAR, which stands for Awareness, Desire, Knowledge, Ability, and Reinforcement.

ADKAR

This is a change management tool used to promote long-lasting individual and organizational change. It was developed by Prosci founder Jeff Hiatt, and I have found it to be very effective.[3] ADKAR is an acronym that represents the five outcomes an individual or organization must achieve for change to be successful and sustainable: awareness, desire, knowledge, ability, and reinforcement. I encourage you to look it up and engage with this great work. Here is a brief summary:

- Awareness (Why do I/we need to change?)
- Desire (Why should I want to change, or what's in it for me?)
- Knowledge (What new knowledge do I need in order to change?)
- Ability (What new abilities, training, or resources do I need in order to change?)
- Reinforcement (What am I positively reinforcing?)

Answer the questions honestly within the model, and this model will help you to change more efficiently and have long-lasting success with the change. As you identify areas of growth and improvement, this model will guide you in processing necessary areas of focus within your change effort.

Change is inevitable, so how you process change is important. In order to harness the power of the Why and Now, you should identify ways to continue learning, growing, and developing in order to enact positive change. When you are focused on achieving more, you look for strategic change.

KEY TAKEAWAYS AND TIPS

p Change is a constant, but how we react to it and how we are proactive with it can have a profound impact on our success.

p Whenever doing something that you have never done, it will be uncomfortable. Embrace the discomfort as long as it aligns with your Why. Too many people run from discomfort and end up in places they didn't desire.

p Having a positive attitude really does matter. The more negative your attitude is, the less likely you are to achieve more. Be realistic, but be positive. Always remember that there are people who would love to have your bad days!

p A great personal or organizational change management tool is ADKAR (Awareness, Desire, Knowledge, Ability, and Reinforcement). This research-based tool will help you have long-lasting, successful change if implemented well.

Chapter 12

IMPACT:
The Principle of Others

Forest Harper: Former Pfizer Senior Executive,
President of INROADS Inc., and Master Mentor

This former Fortune 100 executive turned president of INROADS, an organization to help underrepresented youth obtain internships in Corporate America, sat back and reminisced about one of his great mentors. He is fond of his late uncle, Walter Crenshaw, who was one of the Tuskegee Airmen. Walter passed away in 2016. Forest remembers asking his Uncle Walt a question thirty years ago. He said, "Uncle, how did you live this long, and what is the secret of life?" His uncle responded, "The secret of life is when I am able to answer three questions. One, where I was born. Two, when I was born. Three, why I was born." His uncle stated his Why was to serve others. That moment inspired Forest so much that he says, "Once I heard that, it was simple for me—when I came out of Corporate America, I wanted my work to serve others."

He didn't have to wait until after Corporate America, because while he was there he served so many people, including me. Forest Harper was and continues to be one of my mentors. I first met him during my undergraduate studies, as I was the president of the School of Business Student Leadership Council, and he led our Corporate Alliance Partners. Not only has he been a mentor for me but also for countless others. Forest states, "I tell all of my youth, my purpose of being here at INROADS and being CEO is to serve them. That's the only purpose I have." This purpose of his is evident not only in the time he chooses to give to me and others, but also in how he ended our interview. He stated, "I'm honored to serve!" Forest Harper understands that his impact on others matters. He learned this valuable lesson from good ol' Uncle Walt and Uncle Walt's answer to his three questions. Forest says, "So the Why for me is very easy. It's the ability to give back. If I can give back only one thing, it's servant leadership. And that's the Why!"

Workers perform harder and extend more effort when their work is linked to how it benefits others.

In this chapter, you will learn how focusing on others helps you to act and achieve more. The Principle of Others is a powerful one. Workers perform harder and extend more effort when their work is linked to how it benefits others.

Three studies point to this reality. The first was a study of fund-raisers raising money for student scholarships. Fund-raisers who were randomly assigned to spend five minutes with a scholarship recipient increased their time on the phone with potential donors 142 percent and increased average weekly revenue by 171 percent. Fund-raisers who didn't meet the recipient showed no significant difference in persistence or performance. The second study about pool lifeguards showed that those who read stories of lifeguards saving drowning swimmers perceived their work as more meaningful, which led to an increase in hours and more effort in helping swimmers practice safety behaviors. The last study reported radiologists who saw a picture of a patient they were going to X-ray showed more empathy, wrote 12 percent longer reports, and showed a 46 percent increase in diagnostic findings.[1] Did you just think the same thought I had? If I ever need to go to the radiologist, I am quickly pulling out a picture of me and my family! In these studies, people were not motivated to act simply because they could get something from it, but rather because of the Principle of Others. One way to focus on others is to take a cue from Forest Harper and become a mentor!

MENTORING MATTERS

Mentoring is one of those strange things, like the smile, in that it is a benefit to someone else but it benefits you at the same time. I love those types of win-win situations. When you are a mentor, you have the privilege of helping someone else grow, learning from your mistakes, and accelerating your mentee's learning. Researchers have found that the benefits of mentoring of the mentee are greater career success, development of leadership skills, and increased work performance.[2] Mentoring others can also reduce perceptions of career plateauing, career progress uncertainty, and job monotony. This is important because employees who do have unchallenging jobs or very routine and boring tasks may experience job/contentment plateaus. Mentoring others is one way to reduce perceptions of career plateauing and continue making an impact.

Some people face a professional identity crisis when they feel stuck at work, and mentoring others can help by restoring a sense of positive identity in a role, increasing positive attitudes toward work, and creating a sense of meaningful work. All this comes from helping another human being! I find greater satisfaction in my own work, because of what it financially allows me to do in the realm of mentoring. Part of my Why is mentoring young men without active fathers in their homes so that they will hopefully change the fatherless cycle in their own lives (I grew up mainly without a present father in my life). Making an impact here continues to motivate me to give my best when I work.

Jennifer Eugene understands this concept of mentoring more than most. She has more than thirty years of experience working for and leading a utility company and now manages a diverse team. Jennifer had a challenging time coming through the ranks of utilities, as she was one of only a few women. At her company, she was the first female minority engineer. As she thinks back, she doesn't remember one woman who served as her supervisor. Now, she is a manager and mentor for men and women alike. She states, "I have been able to hire really great talent and help them shape their careers. Mentor them outside of work and do things like that, which really matter. The number-one thing I said was, if I was in a position to lead a team, I would not lead them like I was led." She didn't always feel fully supported, she says. "Part of coaching and mentoring for the next generation is to provide guidance and direction and really make it such that they have someone to lean on and that they have someone that has experiences and can kind of guide them along the way." She credits mentoring as an empowering force that encourages her in her sometimes challenging environment.

Tips for Mentoring

Many workplaces have mentor programs, so you may want to ask what it takes for you to get involved. It is also okay to have a mentee outside of your organization. I have had the privilege of having some amazing mentors in my life, and many of them have exhibited *Forbes'* seven key tasks for mentors. *Forbes* states that mentors should do the following:

1. Develop and manage the mentor relationship: Take the lead and shape the mentor relationship by setting goals and building trust.

2. Sponsor: Open doors and seek out opportunities to expose your mentee to your network.
3. Survey the environment: Assess possibilities and opportunities while looking out for potential landmines for your mentee.
4. Guide and counsel: Be a sounding board and a purveyor of wisdom for your mentee.
5. Teach: Share your knowledge, experiences, and training.
6. Model: Show what it means to be a leader, a productive worker, and a good citizen.
7. Motivate and inspire: Encourage and help your mentee understand how their goals impact the organizational goals.[3]

Tips for Being Mentored

While it is great to have one mentor, realize that you can have multiple mentors based on each person's area of strength. If you are considering asking someone to mentor you, set up a meeting and ask. If the person agrees to be your mentor, it's important to find out how often he or she is willing to meet with you. Let the mentor drive that expectation so that you are not burdensome or overwhelming for him or her.

NOT THE MIRROR THIS TIME

What I mean by "not the mirror this time" is that the focus is not on you or me but on someone else. There is great power in focusing on someone else. There are some people who only focus on other people and not themselves, and they need to treat themselves with the great care and concern they give to others. For the rest of us, we have greater task significance when we focus on others. When people understand that their work adds value to others in or outside the organization, their meaningfulness is enhanced. Not only is meaning impacted, but motivation also improves when an employee is aware of how his or her job affects others.

Understanding that your work adds value to others can enhance meaningfulness.

Of all the people I know and have interviewed, Irene Bailey definitely understands her impact on others. Irene was born in Senegal. Through a series of events and a family tragedy, Irene ended up being placed in an SOS village in Germany. SOS is a global non-profit organization for orphaned and neglected children. Irene's SOS mother ended up raising ten children in total.

Fast-forward, and Irene is now an educational consultant and is passionate about helping youth become victors and not victims. Throughout her life, she said she could have chosen to be a victim of the many challenges she faced, and people would have understood, but she chose to learn from those things to become stronger. She now challenges and inspires others to do the same. Irene states, "It's truly up to us. If you say you are a victim, then yes, you are. If you say that you are a survivor, then you are. It depends on what you believe and what you feed yourself."

Irene didn't just start giving back in adulthood, but she has been doing this since she was a youth. She shared how she grew up in this foster care system as a disadvantaged kid, but in elementary school she would raise money for other disadvantaged kids two to three times a year. Even during her hardships, Irene chose not to focus on the mirror all the time, and that continues with her as an adult. Her impact is powerfully priceless.

Adam Rees started his CrossFit gym out of a need to serve others. He is inspired by his impact on his members but also on the impact that they can have on other people. In thinking about his CrossFit members who have later become coaches, he shares, "They start CrossFit because they enjoy it for whatever reason, but then they see how it benefits other people, and they want to be a part of that change in other people's lives too. Not just their own." While the gym continues to be financially sustainable, Adam says that CrossFit Clinton is not about the money. He is driven by the change he is supporting in other people's lives. He tries his hardest to let not only his coaches but also his members know how much he cares about them and how special they are to him and to the gym.

Focusing on others improves your chances of success and action. As human beings, we have an internal drive to help others, and we tend to feel good about ourselves and our work when we focus on The Principle of Others. Mentoring others and impacting their lives with both your Why and your Now will definitely help you to achieve more.

KEY TAKEAWAYS AND TIPS

p Mentoring others can help you stay motivated and encourage great meaning in your work. It has been proven to help with those who feel stagnant and stuck.

p Focusing on others, in appropriate ways, helps people to achieve more. There are several studies that show that seeing how things benefit others can actually increase effort, focus, and productivity.

p One great way to focus on others is by applying the IMOA concept (Intentional Moments of Appreciation). You can appreciate others with a thoughtful email, a handwritten note, a conversation, or a phone call with detailed and specific appreciation. You can even help a colleague with a project or work. We can do this 365 days a year, but if you want somewhere to start, try it weekly, and at least you would have 52.14 (that's really how many weeks there are in a year) IMOAs.

p When your Why includes a genuine impact on others, you may have just boosted your effort and performance!

Chapter 13

PROMISE:
The What, When, and Who

Nathaniel Benjamin: Retired Air Force and Deputy Chief Human Capital Officer for a Federal Agency

Nathaniel went into the military at seventeen years old. He remembers being at college on September 11 and watching the devastation on the TV screens on campus, then being activated and leaving campus the Saturday after that fateful Tuesday. Being in the military was truly impactful for Nathaniel. He learned a lot about discipline and being a person of action, integrity, and commitment. Nathaniel is truly action and objective focused. When he says he is going to do something, more than likely it will be done. Nathaniel is so focused on fulfilling his promise to be excellent that he plans two meetings with himself a week. He invites himself to his office on Outlook, closes the door, and he works on what he will do, when he will do it, and who he needs in order to do it. Every year he sets objectives and goals for his life. He even has strategic planning meetings with his family twice a month where they talk about everything from day care to cutting the grass to how they are going to prioritize for date night. "I work toward the objective," Nathaniel says. "Everything else that's in the middle is nice; it's context; it's great to know. You use wisdom and use it wisely, and then you move forward to your objectives."

Nathaniel also writes out what he needs to accomplish, because he believes that you further commit to it once you get it out of your head and onto paper. He states, "When you become intentional, you make the effort to do what it is that you've strategized and that you've written so that now you want to execute and implement." He also believes in keeping wise counsel around him to help him stay on course, and even move off course if that isn't the best direction at the time. He calls this group his board of directors. These directors in his life are there to help him on specific issues. Some do not even know they are on his board, but he knows.

In moving to a place of action, Nathaniel not only challenges his own boundaries but also the boundaries of others. "'You can't do it' doesn't really work for me," he says. When someone tells him he can't, he uses that as ammunition to do it. Nathaniel made a promise to this country at seventeen and today makes a promise to his family and those he serves at work and in the community to be truly excellent.

A plan is something that you want to do, whereas a promise is something that you commit to doing.

What is the difference between a plan and a promise? A plan is something that you want to do, whereas a promise is something that you commit to doing. We generally make plans with work colleagues and maybe even dinner plans with another couple, but a promise is usually made with very important people in your life or for a very important occasion. A promise is usually given to family or those like family. While the promises you make will impact your family, they will impact you even more. What will you promise yourself to do practically to live out your Why now? What is holding you back from making that commitment?

WHY ALIGNMENT

If you haven't already gone through the Why exercises, I encourage you to go back to chapter 3 and identify your Why and create your Macro Why Statement (MaWS). This will help guide you as you begin to identify what aligns with your MaWS. Also, what are your most important Micro Whys (e.g., family, career, faith, etc.)? Write out your Micro Whys and your purpose/intent for those areas.

Spend regular time making sure that your actions are in alignment with your Why. You can reflect quarterly, semiannually, or even annually, but make sure you do it on a consistent basis. I call these reflective moments Creative Cocoons, where you are able to flourish with reflection, to think, process, and generate new ideas. While this intentional time to reflect is important, it is also important to wake up every morning connecting to your Why. Whether you say your MaWS to yourself, or you review some of your Why symbols as motivation, you should remain connected to your Why. Even if you are not in a career or calling that you love, remember you can still bring meaning with you to make a difference where you are. So, when is your first Creative Cocoon moment going to be?

WHY STORIES AND SYMBOLS

Tim Hurley: Executive Director of Teach for America Charlotte and Father of Triplets

Tim is pretty busy. He not only leads an organization where he is impacting the lives of new teachers and students, but when he gets home, he is impacting the lives of his amazing triplet children. At work, whenever Tim gets tired, down, or challenged by his work, he will usually pull out his mental Rolodex of one student in particular that he taught. He met this student in his second year of teaching. This student was supposed to be tracked to a special education class, but through a mistake with paperwork, he was put into Tim's non–special education class. Tim had a conversation with the student and his mom, and they all decided to give it a shot and let the student stay in the class. His mom stated, "Well, if you think he can do the work, let's keep him in your class." While it would take this student two to three times longer to do the work, he would always continue and persevere. Tim says, "To this day, when I think of examples of character and courage, I think of this guy. He could do the work, but it would take him two to three times as long. The thing is, he just kept working. He kept on pushing. It's been probably fifteen years since I taught him, but I still think of him on a weekly basis because the kid was awesome. He was just all heart, smart kid, good kid, good character. When I look at my own kids now, I think a lot about . . . I hope they have the kind of character this kid did." Tim consistently reminds himself of this Why story to continue pushing.

Why stories are personal stories throughout your life that remind you and encourage you in your Why.

Like Tim, you need to consistently remind yourself of your Why, and one really great way is through Why stories and symbols. Why stories are personal stories throughout your life that remind you and encourage you in your Why. They can be amazing stories or really challenging stories where you have learned something special. These could be stories of how you have helped someone, provided amazing customer service, or received a special thank-you from a colleague. These stories are specific to you and should be memorable. Each time before a speaking event, I try to run through some of my Why stories to continue to remind myself why I do this amazing work in the first place.

Why symbols can be pictures of people who inspire your Why (mine include my family, Albert Einstein, Pythagoras/Magellan, Thomas Edison and the light bulb, Nelson Mandela, Phiona Mutesi, Nick Vujicic, and my mom, to name a few). What quotes or images capture the essence of your Why? One of my Why symbols is a box without walls because it communicates unseen boundaries. After you have established your Why, consistently keep it before you by framing it, writing it, and surrounding yourself with your Why symbols. Some people, like Kortni Alston, will wear their Why symbols, and others will have them in plain view in their offices, on their phones, or at home.

PMPM: FOUR TYPES OF ACCOUNTABILITY

How will you be held accountable to continue this Why journey? First and foremost, your Why should be so compelling to you that it inspires you to move forward, but it is also helpful to have people who can inspire you and you can inspire them. There are four types of accountability that can help as you move to action. I call these PMPM: Personal, Mentee, Peer, and Mentor.

The first is Personal accountability. This level of accountability focuses on the person in the mirror and what you will do to continue this journey. This can include making sure you have your Creative Cocoon moments or other times of reflection. The second is Mentee accountability. You should inspire someone else with your journey, warts and all. Who can you mentor because it will hold you accountable to continue going after your Why? The third is Peer accountability. This accountability focuses on a friend or someone on the same "level" as you, who can challenge you and inspire you at the same time. The last is the Mentor accountability. This accountability is generally someone who is where you desire to be or at least close to where you want to be and who can inspire you toward greater clarity and action. Out of the PMPM, who are you missing, and what is your promise to secure all four levels of accountability?

YOUR WHY NETWORK

Tonya Moore, PhD: Nurse and Administrator of Community Health Services

In the midst of her demanding doctoral program, Tonya wondered how she would get it all done. She worked full-time, was a full-time single mother, and was in a full-time doctoral program. She was certified, full-time busy. She knew that there was a purpose to doing all she did, and she had to make sacrifices in other areas of her life. Sometimes she didn't have people who understood her journey. There were even some people that she had to temporarily remove from her journey. Tonya says, "It's not that I did not have supporters. My support system did not understand why I was doing these things at that time of my life in trying to achieve my goal. They felt that I should wait or change priorities." There were people who had her best interests in mind but still gave advice without fully understanding her Why. She says, "Sometimes you may have people who are giving you advice when they think that they know every variable, everything that you're doing and why you're doing it. That advice may not align with your goals." One of her biggest supporters and motivators was her son, Ralph, who was a state swim champion and is now attending the United States Naval Academy in Annapolis. She credits his support and a few others that have helped her to achieve more than she even thought was possible. Although her Why network was not always perfect, the fact that they were there was crucial to Tonya and her certified, full-time busy life.

It's not just about what you know but who you know that will support you.

Who is in your Why network? These are people who support and value you and want to see you succeed. These people will encourage you toward living out your Why, Now. There really is a difference between friends and people we simply spend time with. Share your Why with those trustworthy key stakeholders in your life. I do understand that there can be a fear here for some people, because you have been hurt by those who were supposed to support you in the past. Press ahead and find the right people. It doesn't have to be only lifelong friends or family, but it should be people who support you and want to sincerely help you. A great place to also develop this network of people is at work. You can do lunches, after-work events, or simply take initiative to learn about others. For the extroverts this may seem easy, but remember to support your network as well, and don't allow the focus to be only on you. For the introverts this may seem hard, but maybe joining an affinity group or volunteer group can help facilitate closer relationships if you do not prefer to do the above suggestions. If you are not valued by your manager, then make sure you are intentional with reaching out to those who do support you. This could be your closest friends and/or your social media network. It's not just about what you know but who you know that will support you.

IMPLEMENTATION INTENTIONS

What will you ultimately implement? I shared several tips in this book that can help you achieve more through both your Why and your Now. What are the top five things that stood out to you while reading this book? Write them down and rank them in order of importance. Now, focus on one thing at a time and build it into your rhythm. Here are some tips to help turn this dream into action, because there is a big difference between knowledge acquisition and knowledge utilization. The latter will help you move forward.

KEY TAKEAWAYS AND TIPS

p Visualize what a great workday realistically looks like. Not a perfect one, but a realistic one, and give amazing effort.

p Develop implementation intentions. This is when an intention is given goal-directed behaviors, like if-then or when-then statements. Example: "When I get to work first thing in the morning, I will eat my frog of finishing the proposal." Include these three elements in your implementation intentions: the point in time, the place, and the type of action.

p Do your tomorrow list today and include the Principle of the Frog, Step, Seed, and Smile. You will likely feel much more positive and have much more energy toward accomplishing your goals.

p Don't share it with the public unless you expect accountability! Public recognition of what you would like to accomplish can give a premature sense of accomplishment.

Conclusion

So how does it feel? You just finished this book that was focused on you! You have clarified your Why (both Macro and Micro), you have learned how to give your all now and be "On 10," and you have learned how to find the intersection of both your Why and your Now. You no longer have to bounce back and forth, struggling to balance out purpose and productivity—now you can ultimately achieve more! You have learned how to reflect, give more effort, and be more productive. My hope for you going forward is that you would continue to apply the practical tools I shared in this book and share this message with those who could use a little Why and Now.

Dive into the addenda for additional tips and tools to help you grow personally and be a better leader based on my *Your Why Matters Now* research. If you want to engage in the continuing conversation, you can join the mailing list at www.workmeaningful.com to receive additional resources and relevant updates on workplace engagement and diversity & inclusion. There you will find additional insights and research that will help you live out your WHY and NOW. *Your Why Matters Now* journey is just beginning, and I encourage you to enjoy it in your pursuit to achieve more!

Let me ask a question: What will you do? No matter how tough things get for your Why and Now, they are worth fighting for. I am reminded of an interview I conducted with the former NFL player Kelly Jennings. In ending the interview and discussing action and sometimes being afraid to move, he said, "Go! Because that's what I learned in football. It could be rain or sleet. You see rain in football games. You are still going to play. It doesn't matter, and this time you are sitting in the locker room, saying to yourself,

'It's cold out there. I do not want to go play.' Sometimes it turns out to be your best game in the worst weather!" Allow whatever moment Now is to be your best game as you approach the field of your life and work with both your Why and Now. Give it your all. Do not stop; do not quit; do not ever give up! As the ancient philosopher Lao Tzu said, "The journey of a thousand miles begins with one step."

30 Practical Tips to Professionally and Personally Achieve More

Here is a list of thirty tips that you can utilize to help you in your journey of achieving more. Several of these items are listed in the book, and some are not. Some of the tips will require a look back at the book to dig deeper, but others are stand-alone tips that you can start today. Do not get overwhelmed by this list, but identify one or two things that you can immediately start to work on.

Purposeful Effort

1. **Write Out Your Why Statement and Remind Yourself Consistently:** The foundation of all of this is to know why you are doing something. Utilize chapter 3 to create Macro and Micro Why statements using the "I in order to__" format. Print out your Why statement, save it as your screensaver, put it on notecards and keep it in your car, frame it, or do whatever it takes to see it consistently. [Chapter 3]

2. **Get Excited at Work:** Engage in job crafting, where you find something that excites and energizes you, and find a way to do it at work. For example, if you like to give back, then volunteer to lead a volunteer group or sign up people to serve for a worthy cause. [Chapter 4]

3. **Identify Your "On 10" Behaviors:** What do you normally do when you are giving your best and hitting on all cylinders? What are the environmental cues and things that are happening for you to give everything you choose to give? Remember: this is not about

what other people do, but what you choose to do at your very best. [Chapter 5]

4. **Practice the Principle of the Frog, Step, Seed, and Smile:** *Frog*: Do the most challenging task first thing in the day or in the week. *Step*: Make progress, even incrementally, in something that has great meaning for you. *Seed*: Each day/week schedule time to learn something about your craft or industry; for instance, read a blog, listen to a podcast, watch a webinar, read a chapter of a book, read a journal article, or something that works for you. *Smile*: Implement IMOAs (Intentional Moments of Appreciation) where you seek out opportunities to thank others and appreciate them with thank-you notes, a phone call, a thoughtful email, a special gift, or something else that expresses appreciation. [Chapter 8]

Productivity

5. **Don't Manage Your Time, Lead It:** Many people simply manage their time, which is essentially acknowledging where time went versus telling your time where to go. It is similar to budgeting. True budgeting is not asking at the end of the month, "Where did my money go?" but at the beginning of the month, telling your money where to go! At the beginning of the week, plan out your week, putting in the most important things first. Every morning look over your schedule and make sure it accurately depicts what you want to do. Be flexible but try to stick to your schedule. Don't forget to include an hour for a little personal growth time in there as well.

6. **Do a Tomorrow List Today:** At the end of a workday or before you go to bed, identify what you need to accomplish the next day and put it in your schedule (see next tip). Don't wait until tomorrow to identify what is truly priority and what needs to be done.

7. **Stop Doing To-Do Lists and Start Scheduling Your Items:** This works together with the previous tip. I'm sorry, but to-do lists hardly work, and unless it is in your calendar and given a specific time, it is

less likely to be done. If what you have to do is really important, you can find a time to actually complete it.

8. **Focus on To-Go Versus To-Date Updates:** Telling yourself how far you have come can actually decrease your drive and motivation and can give a premature sense of accomplishment. When you focus on what's to go, it is more motivating to finish. (For example, it is better to say, "Out of the twenty items, I only have twelve more to go," versus "I've already done eight.")

9. **Don't Check Email When You First Get to Work:** I know, I know . . . but you have to. Actually, most people do not have to check their email first thing. What if you scheduled 25, 50, or 90 minutes to work on your most challenging project or task that day (the Frog) and then checked your email? With the thousands of emails we get every day, it can be easy to fall into the email trap and make things unnecessarily urgent. If you feel you have to, then before you get to the office, scan your emails to address whether anything is absolutely urgent. If it is, take care of that email and that email alone. If it is not, focus on your Frog and then check email. If you want to go even further, schedule times to check your email. During work hours, I usually check my email only two or three times, and I have definitely turned off the addictive email ding!

10. **Use DND and Airplane Mode:** Many business travelers will tell you that their most productive time is when they are in flight. Why? They cannot accept phone calls and for the most part they are in Airplane mode. When an assignment or project needs great focus, use the Do Not Disturb mode or Airplane mode on your phone. What I like about DND is that if it is really important, a person can call twice (if you have that feature) and it will send that caller through. Airplane mode is when I truly need to focus and need to limit distractions. You will see just how productive you are when you minimize the alerts, calls, news updates, emails, and text messages you receive every day.

11. **Have a PrAP:** A PrAP is a Professional Accountability Partner. This is a like-minded person who is a peer and who will hold you accountable to achieving your professional goals. I meet with my PrAP once a month, and we talk about our goals and leave each meeting with one goal to accomplish by the next meeting. Think of it as your gym buddy who makes sure you work out when you don't feel like it. Your PrAP will drive your achievement and productivity up if you both commit to one another.

Rest and Recovery

12. **Focus on Your Energy and Not Just Efficiency:** Yes, it is important to focus on efficiency at work and in your life, but what if you had more effort and brainpower to give? That more comes from focusing on your energy. If you fuel your body with healthy nutrition, exercise, sleep, and rest, you can help yourself with managing emotions and focusing. Eat healthy, exercise three to five times a week, sleep at least seven hours, and take strategic fifteen- to thirty-minute naps throughout the day at your low-energy times.

13. **Identify Effective Recovery Strategies:** It is helpful to develop a rhythm of how you work. There are several different techniques, but find the right one for you. There is the Pomodoro technique, where you work a 25-minute burst, take a 5-minute break, and then work another 25-minute burst. There is also the 50/10 or 90/15 method, where you work for 50 minutes and take a 10-minute break, or you work for 90 minutes and take a 15- to 20-minute break. Depending on the complexity of my day, I have used all three at different times. Also, take your lunch and don't eat it at your computer. When you work, you deplete your energy sources and need to recover. The law of diminishing returns shows we have a limited amount of energy and effort to give each day, and that's why smart people don't work harder—they recover well to work smarter.

Learning Mindset

14. **Conduct a Gap Analysis:** Understand where your essential gaps exist. You can simply ask "Where am I now?" and "Where do I want to be?" and identify what it will take to fill the gap to bring those two together. It's not just about your motivation but also your ability to get to your desired outcome. For example, if you wanted to receive a promotion, it would be helpful to know what the requirements are for that promotion or new position. Do you need more training, education, and/or experience? Do you need a mentor to help you understand the hidden norms that people at the level operate by? Once you understand where you are and what it takes to get to where you want to go, you can then create a plan to fill your gaps.

15. **Focus More on Learning than Performance:** One of the biggest challenges that many people face is that we have been conditioned to have a performance mindset versus a learning mindset. When you have a performance mindset, the focus is only on how you did. When you have a learning mindset, the focus is on how you grew and developed as well as how you did. Ask yourself questions such as "What did I learn?" "How can I do better?" and "What key lessons can I gain from my failures?" People who focus on learning tend to continue to get better in the long run and surpass those who are solely concerned with their performance.

16. **Embrace Failure as Fuel:** I know that we hear this all the time. But it is so vital to our growth and development. Some people are crushed by failure. Let's be honest: most people aren't walking around excited about their failure. However, there are those who are paralyzed by it and those who use it as a data point to get better. Think of a time you have failed in the past and were better for it later. Now, put your energy less into how horrible you feel after you have failed and more into how you can use it to do better next time. *Those who are not failing are simply not trying hard enough!*

17. **Try New Things:** Do things you have no expertise in and haven't mastered in order to learn and grow. There is a spillover effect of growing in areas where you are not experienced. That process of learning spills over into your work and life and helps you to adapt to change and take on new things more easily. Every year I do something that I have never done so that I am constantly learning new things. You can take a painting class, a cooking class, climb a mountain, run a marathon, create a Lego masterpiece, or go to a lecture on an unfamiliar topic. Whatever you do, maximize the gains from learning something new.

18. **Find a Workplace Mentor:** Having a mentor is vital, even if he or she isn't in your specific workplace. A mentor can show you your blind spots and weaknesses. A mentor can help you understand how to get better and improve. You do not necessarily only need one mentor, but you can have several that may help you with different aspects of your growth. One huge tip is to ask what is a realistic frequency they can meet with you. Let them be honest and give you timelines that work for them. Many mentor relationships can be once a month, once every other month, quarterly, and maybe even twice a year. Anything less than that is more of an advisor.

19. **Find an Achievement Hobby:** What you do during nonwork hours is almost as important as what you do during work hours. It is here that there is also a spillover effect to your work. When you have a hobby where you are able to achieve, you take those same psychological benefits with you to work. Possible achievement hobbies include baking, cooking new meals, running, hiking, cycling, competing in triathlons, building furniture, reading a book, creating art work, and so on. These are activities that have a start and a completion.

20. **Take Ownership and Initiative:** There are generally two types of people. There are those that life happens to, and those that happen to life. The first is a reactive person and the second is a proactive person who tries to find ways to accomplish new tasks or get more

done. The first type of person waits for things to be given to them, and the second type of person asks for things to be given to them. One practical way to take ownership and initiative is when you finish early on a task or project (I know it happens sometimes in life), identify what more you can do or ask for more to do. Another way is to take ownership of your learning and development and don't simply wait for your manager or supervisor to tell you what you should do to learn and grow. Even if you cannot go to training, you can read a book, watch a webinar, or listen to a podcast. Yes, you can even do this during nonwork times, because after all, this is about your growth and development. A little ownership and initiative could do you some good!

Appreciative Attitude

21. **Be a Practical Optimist, Not an Impractical One:** Practical optimists are positive and believe they can achieve their goals, but they are practical about what it will take to get there, including the challenges, obstacles, time, resilience, and effort needed. An impractical optimist thinks he can do anything easily. Many times he may underestimate what it takes to do something while he overestimates his ability to get it done. Think about a sports team that underestimates their opponent and is stunned in a loss. One practical way to be a practical optimist (see what I did there) is to believe you can achieve something but think through how much time it will realistically take you and possible obstacles you may face. Apply the Four-Stage Analysis Model, or as I like to call them, the Four Questions: Where am I now? Where do I want to be? What are the barriers preventing me from getting there? How can the barriers be removed?

22. **Practice the Art of Reframing:** Reframing is simply when you take a situation and think about how you can learn from it or what you can do to grow. When challenging things happen to me, many times I say to myself, "There are people who would love to have my bad days." My car stopped one day on the side of the road and I was

mad. I started to calm myself down by thinking and saying to myself how grateful I was to even have a car to break down. Sometimes when you are having a bad day at work, think about the millions who are unemployed and would love to have your "bad" job. Reframing helps me funnel my energy into good places versus being drained by my own inner negativity.

Communication/Feedback

23. Turn Nos into Yeses: When you are told no at work, what do you do? Do you simply say, "Okay," or do you ask for feedback to get to a yes later, or learn why you shouldn't ask for that in the first place? I remember being told no by my school where I was obtaining my MBA. I asked to speak to the new students and they said no. I was crushed, but I humbled myself and went back and asked them what I could do to eventually get them to a yes, and I have spoken for my MBA alma mater at least three times since that first no. It doesn't always work out that way, and sometimes learning from a no from one person/organization may get you a yes with another. I even learned this principle with my kids, as they constantly tell me no and I have to share the "why" with them and kindly ask them to do it "now!" Still a work in progress.

24. **Be Vulnerable and Ask for Help:** Share success and failures with those you trust and others you think can benefit. You are vulnerable when you realize you don't have it all together and can ask for help. It is okay to need people and a big thing for those who achieve more is vulnerability and asking for help! Regularly ask people to give you honest feedback (both positive and painful). Some people call it a Stop Continue Start (SCS) or a Plus/Delta (see next tip). You don't need to be a fake hero, because smart heroes utilize the people and resources around them to get a task done. *You are not stupid because you do not know something. You are stupid when you do not know and still do not ask! Be smart, not stupid!*

25. **Seek Feedback, Don't Wait for It:** Many people wait for their leaders to give them feedback, but those who achieve more seek out meaningful feedback from their leaders, peers, and their direct reports. Conduct a simple Plus/Delta where you ask, "What am I doing well?" and "What do I need to change or improve?" You can do this on a monthly or quarterly basis, but don't wait until your annual evaluation to find out how you are doing. Take ownership and initiative by asking for constructive feedback.

Professional Development

26. **Ask For/Take on Challenging Assignments:** One practical way people can grow is in developmental assignments where skills are grown in other areas. This allows you to be ready for promotions. It also increases your competency in another area, which makes you more marketable. I had been speaking for years when I started my consulting business. When I first started, it was terrifying, as I had never done this before, but I was excited to take on the challenge and serve my clients well. Those around you will see your initiative and will likely take notice of your effort.

27. **Create Your Personal Reward System:** Set up a reward system after a big project or phase of a project or accomplishment. This could include a trip, extra money to spend, or a special dinner. When you reward yourself with something meaningful, it helps to keep you motivated. I remember I needed to finish a phase of my book project, and I told my daughter Lydia that when I finished that phase, we could go out to our normal dinner spot. I finished that phase and we had an amazing dinner. That reward kept me looking forward to it. What can you reward yourself with?

28. **Consume High-Quality Content Consistently:** There are high-quality consumers, and no, I do not mean they exclusively shop on Rodeo Drive, but the types of information they consume are high-quality. What content are you consuming? Low-quality content

can be TV shows, certain reality TV shows, and social media at large. High-quality content can include reality TV shows that help you, such as *The Prophet* or *Shark Tank* (I get great business ideas as an entrepreneur). High-quality content can also be podcasts or books that can help you develop and grow. Leaders truly are readers, so what are you reading? Those who produce high-quality content usually consume high-quality content. Think about it like fuel. For what you want to accomplish in life, are you consuming more of the right type of fuel that will get you there, or fuel that has the potential to mess up your engine?

29. **Develop Your Board of Directors:** Who are the people in your life that you turn to when you have questions? Who advises you when you have important decisions to make? It is important to clearly identify these people and talk to them on a regular basis (monthly, quarterly, yearly). Some board members are ad hoc, meaning as they are needed they should be contacted. Many times people will not know they are on your board of directors, but identify who in your life can help you in the areas that are vital to you. They should be excelling in their area of expertise. [Chapter 12]

30. **Join an Organization or Attend an Industry Conference:** Is your industry associated with a trade organization? It is important to keep up-to-date on what is happening in your industry and sphere of work. Even if you don't have anything local, what are the national organizations that support your line of work? As a speaker I am involved with the National Speakers Association, and as an HR professional I am involved with both SHRM and AHRD. Get your industry publications and identify if you can attend their local, regional, or national conferences. It is up to you how much you grow or don't grow, and industry associations and conferences can be a really good way to grow and develop your network.

30 Practical Tips
to Achieve More as a Leader

I seem to get one question a lot when presenting my Your Why Matters Now concept, and that is, "How do I inspire my team, employees, or those I lead with this information?" While this book is not focused on how leaders lead with their Why and Now, I wanted to provide some helpful tips that I sometimes share in my "Legendary Leadership" presentation. These tips are broken into key concept areas. Don't feel overwhelmed by the tips, but rather identify one or two that you can begin to do now and put it in your calendar to make progress. While it is important for people to motivate themselves, it is also important for leaders to create an environment where engagement can thrive.

Culture/Inner Work Life

1. **Answer the Two Questions:** As a leader you should know the answer to these two questions for everyone you directly lead: Why did you join our organization/industry in the first place? and What does a successful experience look like to you? If you don't know why they joined, how will you help to motivate and encourage a healthy and positive inner work life? If you don't know what success looks like to them, how will you ever help them get there or reset expectations if their "success" is not possible? Challenge yourself to write the answers down and periodically review them for those you lead. When I was a radio show host, I had a producer who didn't seem very engaged. One day I found out what he wanted to do, which was to eventually have his own show. I could have figured

every way to stifle his dream, but instead I gave up one show a month so that he could have his own segment on my show. He was happier, more engaged, and could tell I cared about his success and not just my own. I have countless stories where I didn't get this right too!

2. **Make Sure Systems Support Collaborative Goals:** Do your systems support collaborative goals? Employees who work as teams with a specific team goal, rather than as individuals only trying to accomplish an individual goal, have higher productivity. Sometimes our systems hurt our collaborative desire. I worked for one organization that said they wanted collaboration, but our bonuses were still tied solely to our individual contributions. When things were really busy, people turned to their individual tasks instead of finding ways to better collaborate.

3. **Believe in the Best of Your Employees:** In a 1968 study by Rosenthal and Jacobson, they told teachers that a selected group of students (who were chosen randomly) would exhibit unusual growth and were highly gifted. The researchers later found that those students displayed greater intellectual development than the students who were not stated as special and highly gifted. Moral: what you believe about your employees will probably come true. These teachers thought that these students had high ability, and when the students failed, they would attribute it more to their effort than their ability. It is also important not to overgeneralize or judge a person's ability or worth based on a single event or action. They really could have been having a bad day and didn't bring their "A" game. Like any good research, a sufficient sample size is needed to make a smart decision.[1]

4. **Courageously Deal with Crisis:** How you deal with a crisis is important. It is important not to rush to judgment and point fingers or place blame. As a leader, find the real issue and develop an action plan to move forward. Remember: normally it is important to praise in public and criticize in private.

5. **Encourage Appropriate Risk-Taking:** Encourage appropriate risk-taking and reward for lessons learned. Sheryl Sandberg once worked for Google. She confessed to the CEO that she had made an error because of a risk she had taken, and the owner said, "I'm so glad you made this mistake, because I want to run a company where we are moving too quickly and doing too much, not being too cautious and doing too little. If we don't have any of these mistakes, we're just not taking enough risk." That statement from the leader says it all. Help people challenge the "normal" in your organization in order to continue growing. Without risks, normal will never be disrupted!

6. **Help People Fail Forward:** When people take the risk, they just might fail. Help them fail forward. Don't just reward outcomes and effort, but also reward learning and progress. This will help people see the process that helped them, such as trying new strategies, getting input from others, and learning from failures in order to move forward efficiently. Give your employees the space to fail because if you are not encouraging effort that may lead to a level of failure, then you are minimizing access to flow and to unlocking your employees' potential at work! My first internship was for Enterprise Rent-A-Car, and my branch manager met with me when I first started and told me that it was okay to make smart mistakes. These were mistakes that were well-thought-out but didn't pan out. This allowed me to be creative and come up with processes and ideas that positively impacted our branch. His guidance allowed me to win a sales award each summer I interned with them.

7. **Minimize or Erase the Politics:** If a person feels that they are playing a highly political game and that they must be overly protective of themselves and their ideals, then they will expend effort and energy in those areas. This decreases the amount of effort for flow, productivity, and creativity. Talk to your team or have them anonymously share how they feel about the level of corporate politics, and seek to disengage your team or project from it. Trust me: you are losing money if your workers are engaged in politics.

8. **Create a Positive Culture:** A positive workplace has these characteristics:

   - Being cared for, being interested in, seeing colleagues as
     friends
   - Providing support for one another and helping others when
     they are struggling
   - Avoiding blame and forgiving mistakes
   - Inspiring each other at work
   - Emphasizing meaning of the work
   - Working with respect, gratitude, trust, and integrity[2]

9. **Intentionally Focus on One Employee Per Week/Month:** Go
   out of your way for people in general, but focus on one employee
   per week or per month. Take them out to lunch and really get to
   know them. Also, figure out a way to do something special for them
   in their project or task, and sacrifice a little of your time to show you
   care for them and their work. When leaders are self-sacrificing, their
   employees are inspired to be more loyal and committed.

10. **Focus on Giving More to Your People than Getting More
    from Your People:** Stop trying to get more out of your people and
    start trying to invest more into your people. There is an unspoken
    and sometimes spoken agreement between organizations and their
    employees that says each will try to get the most out of the other, as
    fast as possible, and then move on without looking in the rearview
    mirror. What if you figured out their interests, hobbies, and motiva-
    tions, and you supported them in those areas? If they became a new
    parent, would you get them a book on parenting, or if they started
    coaching their child's team, would you try to stop by one of the
    games? Show them that you care for them!

11. **Have Courageous Curiosity and Engage in Authentic Listen-
    ing:** These are two things I learned from the kid on the plane who
    wouldn't shut up. Courageous curiosity is when we are genuinely
    interested in someone else and we ask about her or him. Authentic

listening is deeper than active listening. You can fake active listening. You can repeat what the person said, and you can even lean in. When you engage in authentic listening, your questions are relevant and show thought about what the person is saying. Know more about those you lead than what positions they hold or what they can do for you. Know about them!

12. **Help Cultivate Flow:** Allow your employees to periodically turn off email/email notifications; have fewer, more focused meetings; and focus on smaller pieces of their work. Some organizations have even implemented "No Meetings" times to encourage people to do focused work and create an environment where flow can more readily happen.

Meaningful Work

13. **Give Appropriate Autonomy:** Where can you give autonomy and allow people to achieve results? Even if they don't achieve the intended results, will you allow them to follow up with ways they could improve? A summary of Daniel Pink's book *Drive* defines autonomy this way: "Autonomy is different from independence. It means acting with choice—which means we can be both autonomous and happily interdependent with others."[3] You can increase autonomy by including people in decision making. You can also increase autonomy by helping people understand what they do, when they do it, who they do it with, and how they do it.

14. **Help People See Meaning in Their Work:** People have more creativity, productivity, and energy when their inner work lives (thoughts and feelings they have about work) are positive. Are you helping your employees see how their roles/tasks/projects are contributing and making meaning? Help your employees cross the 5 Why Bridges at work! [Addendum C]

15. **Connect People's Work to Organizational Goals:** Are the most strategic objectives communicated down the line? When employees

know and buy into the strategic organizational goals, they can use this information to job craft in such a way that it is helpful to the organization and organizational effectiveness. How are you linking the tasks, projects, and organizational values to the individual's values to help uncover meaning? Teams that have greater clarity about what they are doing, the scope of their task, and why it matters to the team, organization, and customers have greater progress than the teams without that clarity.

16. **Highlight the Impact the Work Has on Others:** This can increase perceptions of task significance, but people must really believe that their work impacts other people. A study was done where new fundraisers received task significance cues (i.e., how their work impacted scholarship students), and the new fund-raisers showed higher performance their first week on the job than other new fund-raisers who did not receive those same cues.[4]

17. **Be Responsive and Facilitate Interesting and Challenging Work:** Leaders who facilitate interesting and challenging work decrease turnover and absenteeism. Also, leaders and organizations who foster an environment that is responsive to employees' input and values will have employees who are more adaptable, committed to the organization, and who funnel their energies and inspiration toward organizational success. In Ken Blanchard's Situational Leadership 2 Model, he talks about those that are Self-Reliant Achievers who, if left in that stage too long, can regress to Disillusioned Learners. One way to help Self-Reliant Achievers is with a stretch assignment.

Rewards

18. **Give Unexpected, Tangible Rewards:** Give tangible rewards unexpectedly so that people don't associate the reward simply with doing the task. The intangible rewards of praise and positive feedback are normally better than tangible rewards, because every type of expected tangible reward made based on performance (e.g., a

company watch) undermines intrinsic motivation. Praise people with meaningful information on their effort and decision-making and less on specific outcomes. As leaders we should be intentionally looking for opportunities to deliver unexpected rewards.

19. **Make Employee Reward Programs about Recognition and Not Awards:** Employee reward programs work best when they're not about the award but rather about the recognition. More than people like physical items, they like the recognition and pride that come with being Employee of the Month, Worker of the Year, or celebrated in front of their peers. The awards are icing on the cake, but how employees are recognized (e.g., in front of the All-Employee Meeting) is more important.

Communication/Feedback

20. **Check In with People, Don't Check Up on People:** How you approach your check-ins with those you lead is important. When you check up on people, it appears as if you do not trust them, which can create angst among your employees or team. When you check in, you are looking for pertinent updates and how you can help your employee do better. When you check in with people, you offer substantive help or encouragement. Also, if something is going wrong, try to find a solution instead of trying to place personal blame. Set clear, strategic goals during your meetings, but allow members to plan with you and figure out how to meet the goals instead of simply being told exactly what to do.

21. **Know How and When to Praise:** When praising people, make it specific and focus on how they are reaching goals or positively impacting the organization. The timing is the most important aspect of praising them. You need real progress and effort on work for a person to feel the praise was warranted. Without that, people may feel suspicious about your praise. People don't need cuddly little pats on the back every day—they need progress praise. Do you praise your employees, or do you progress praise your employees?

22. **Give Effective Feedback:** When giving feedback, don't over-generalize or judge a person's ability or worth based on a single event or action. Feedback is essential, as it helps people know how they are doing, and it helps people understand how to adjust in order to improve. Do not wait until the annual performance review to give feedback, but give it periodically at monthly or quarterly one-on-one meetings.

23. **Respond Constructively:** Imagine an employee comes to you and shares that he or she finished a recent project. Author Martin Seligman explains four ways to respond to information, and I've added a fifth way. Some of these are not so good, and others help your employees feel valued.

    - *Active constructive*: authentic and enthusiastic support ("That's amazing. How did it feel to finish your project? What did you learn in the process?")
    - *Passive constructive*: positive surface reaction ("I am glad for you . . . ")
    - *Passive destructive*: ignoring what happened ("I got an email yesterday from Jan about happy hour.")
    - *Active destructive*: pointing out the negative ("You do realize that because you are done with the project, we can give you another one, which might be harder.")[5]
    - *Active shifting* (I added this one): shifting his or her story to yours immediately ("I remember when I finished my project a couple of weeks ago. I felt great.")

24. **Create a Safe Environment for People to Give Honest Feedback:** Do your employees feel safe with you and feel that they can talk to you? In many organizations I work with, employees don't feel that they can be honest with their feedback for fear of retaliation, so instead they keep their real comments to themselves or share with other employees they trust. If employees feel like this in your organization, then you are not getting real input but filtered input. While you begin to address the culture and help people know that

their honest and real feedback is valued, you may want to use a temporary, anonymous way for people to share how things are going. Whether the feedback is anonymous or not, it is important that you follow up on that feedback. Share either why you are going to use their feedback or why you are not going to use it. Without the follow-up, people will feel as if what they have to say does not matter.

25. **Seek to Be More Interested Than Interesting:** Is it more important for you to show how impressive you are or show others how impressed you are with them? Show others that you are interested in their lives, their thoughts, and that you care about them being engaged. When you communicate, remember to focus on the person in front of you, because who do people like to talk about the most? You guessed right—themselves!

Motivation

26. **Set Goals with People, Not for People:** When a person sets a goal for themselves or is a part of a goal-setting process, it is normally well received, but when the goal is simply imposed upon people, it can have harmful long-term effects. Allow your members to participate in the goal-setting process. Studies have shown that when an employee participates, there is a positive association with satisfaction, performance, and productivity. Goal commitment and task performance are enhanced when a person believes that they can do it, and they view the person who gave them the goal positively. So help your employees see how the goal is challenging but also one they can achieve.

27. **Motivate Your Employees, Don't Move Them:** Are you moving or motivating your employees? Movement can happen begrudgingly, but motivation happens with energy and excitement. The difference between your employees feeling like they *have to* versus feeling like they *get to* is in how you motivate them. Are you giving your employees a "kick in the butt," which usually leads to movement and not motivation? True motivation is not simply moving your cat

with your foot to try to get it to do something. Because to keep the cat moving, you will have to keep moving the cat with your foot. Real motivation happens when you no longer need to recharge your employees' batteries because they have gotten a generator to keep recharging themselves. No external stimulation is needed, as they desire to do it! When you move your employees, they are focused on achieving the stated goals; when you motivate your employees, they are focused on achieving the stated and unstated goals that lead to growth.[6]

28. **Avoid the External Driving Forces of Demotivation:** Some external driving forces of demotivation include unfair policies, under-appreciation, perceived favoritism, not being listened to, and lack of growth opportunities.[7]

29. **Motivate People Even in Uninteresting Work:** Let's face it: not everything at work is going to be amazing. Motivate people by telling them why the work, project, or activity is necessary and important to do. If you cannot identify this, then maybe you should reconsider if it should be done. Also try building interest in the activity by making a game out of it or finding a way to build team morale with the activity.

30. **Help Your People Implement the Principle of the Frog, Step, Seed, and Smile:** Four things can help improve a person's perceptions of their work: the Frog, Step, Seed, and Smile. When people practice these on a daily or weekly basis, they can help the positivity, effort, and impact of their work. [Chapter 9]

The 5 Why Bridges
at Work

"Why did the worker cross the bridge? Yes, to find deeper meaning in his work."

I know it is a bad and corny joke, but it is true. In my workshops and presentations, my participants and their leaders wanted a practical way to help people find their Micro Why at work, so I created a tool to help them bring meaning, significance, and impact to their current job. This tool is the 5 Why Bridges at Work.

A few important notes about the 5 Why Bridges at Work. The 5 Why Bridges are Self/Family, Team, Customer/Client, Organization, and Community. They are called bridges because they help bridge the gap between the worker having little to no meaning at work and having meaning at work. The worker must choose to intentionally "cross" each bridge and take a more active role in making their work matter and their work experience more positive. When a worker crosses the bridge, they are simply making a choice to identify how that area may give them meaning at work. This metaphoric crossing will help derive meaning at work. Many people try to find meaning in their work, but they should also bring meaning to their work. Your work may have clearly defined ways that the employees find meaning, but you should still bring meaning with you and identify ways you can have meaningful work. These 5 Why Bridges at Work will help you do that. Without them people will likely fall into the sea of meaningless work and feel like they are drowning. When a person crosses one of the five bridges, they are creating a better work experience and thinking more positively about their work, which leads to better work and finding ways to engage their Why at work.

Not everyone will be able to cross all 5 Why Bridges, but you should try as hard as you can to identify if you are able to intentionally cross (find meaning) in each one. This is the only section I am going to ask you to do some math, so you may want a piece of paper and a calculator. Also, challenge your attitude, especially if you do not see your work as favorable (which we will dive into later in this addendum), because again, this is less about you finding meaning in your work and more about you bringing meaning to your work. This tool was inspired by my consulting, hours of research, personal experience, and a few key articles. Let's bring meaning and cross those bridges!

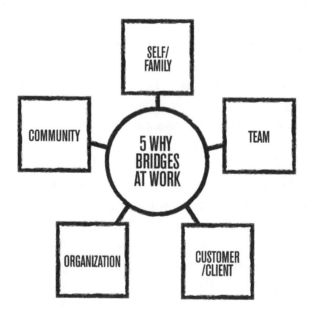

The 5 Why Bridges at Work Tool

Before we get into the tool, here's a breakdown of the 5 Why Bridges:

1. *Self/Family:* You as an individual, your family, personal growth, developing competencies, learning, etc.
2. *Team:* Your team, employees/members you have a direct impact with, any project teams you're a part of
3. *Customer/Client:* The user of your product or service
4. *Organization:* Employees/members you have an indirect impact on, the organization as a whole
5. *Community:* Local and global community

Here is how you use the tool:

- Write out each bridge on a piece of paper. You will rank each bridge in two categories: Importance and Motivating Factor at work. Importance is defined by what is the most important to you at work (where you provide meaning, significance, and value) and what has the most meaning to you. When you think about the five areas at work, which would you rank as most important? Rank that bridge a 5 and then the next bridge a 4, and so on. Motivating Factor is defined by what motivates you the most at work when you think about it. What gives you energy and excites you. This may be the same as your importance ranking or it could be different. Rank the bridge that gives you the most energy and excites you the most a 5, then rank the other bridges accordingly.
- Then multiply your rankings together. (Scores range from 1 to 25; if you get 37, you may want to use a calculator!) You will get your "Why Score at Work," which will help you identify what bridges to focus on to give you that boost of energy and sense of purpose at work. The top score should be an area that you focus on and consistently remind yourself of.

Let me give a fictitious example:

Bridge	Importance	Motivating Factor	Why Score at Work (Importance × Motivating Factor)
Self/Family	5	2	10
Team	3	4	12
Customer/Client	4	5	20
Organization	2	1	2
Community	1	3	3

Now take your top two Why Scores at Work, and these are the areas where you need to focus more at work, because these specific bridges are more important and meaningful and they motivate you. These areas are going to keep motivating you, if you are intentional, when times get tough and when you are having a challenging day. Based on the example, the highest Why score at work is the Customer/Client and the Team. You may be wondering, "What do I do next?" I'm glad you asked!

Next, you want to develop consistency with reminding yourself why this bridge is so vital for bringing meaning to your work. You may have a letter from a client, a customer you helped, or an end user for whom you solved a really hard technical problem. Most of us have that one story that, when recalled, really drives us. Consistently look at that letter, review that email, or ponder that story as a way to continue bringing meaning to your work.

I remember speaking at a conference for social workers, and after the event I received a Facebook message from one of the participants. She shared:

Hi Justin . . . I felt that I needed to tell you how much I appreciated not just your speech but the message you shared. As a social worker, I often feel burnt out after trying to help young individuals but feeling as though I am not succeeding. This has made me question my career choice, however I always knew this is what I was born to do. I attended the symposium yesterday to learn, but also to get out of the office! I really needed to hear your message and feel re-inspired, and I did. Not many people can do your job and do it well. I felt a bit skeptical when you first started out but was then drawn to the message as it hit so close to home. So, I just wanted to say thank you. You are very gifted and I appreciate you sharing that gift with us yesterday.

Have you stopped crying yet? Man, every time I read that letter, I get choked up. I may have a presentation that I didn't think was super amazing and I remember this or review this message. These are those Why moments when I realize why my work is important and what it is all really about. No number of standing ovations will top these moments for me. What's your moment(s)?

Maybe you should frame that thank-you note you received from the CEO (organizational Why bridge), or keep that keepsake from the training you attended as a reminder of how your work is helping you grow (self/family Why bridge), or remember the story when you helped your team complete a huge project and you went above and beyond and your team recognized you for it (team Why bridge). Whatever it is, find your Why symbol or story and go back over it weekly, monthly, or quarterly. Heck, if you are having a really challenging season, you may need a reminder of your Why at work daily! This does not mean that you ignore the other areas that you ranked; it just means that you want to focus on the one or two that have the highest Why scores.

Acknowledgments

I am first and foremost thankful to the Lord, who I believe has given me the ability, creativity, and perseverance to write this book. Bigger than anything, my faith in you is my umbrella Why! Thank you to my amazing business manager, Dari, because without your help I would not have been able to write this book, let alone get away for moments at a time for the many months of research and writing. You have helped so much, and I hope this is worth it. Thanks to my amazing Mom-e who always (well, almost always) let me ask Why! I would also like to thank a few people who were integral in my many, many rough drafts. Marlon and Ardyn Barton, you all have elevated the level of this book, and I am grateful for our many calls (even while your baby was crying in the background). I cannot repay the sacrifices you made to help me (well, maybe at Granny's!). I would like to appreciate Karyn Okelo, DD, Curtis Brown, Anthony Gorrity, Dr. Charlie Wingard, Mrs. Washington, Ken Patterson, and Dominique Ekong for reviewing the book. Jeanette Jordan, you continue to amaze me—thank you for connecting me with so many great people I could interview.

I would like to thank those who allowed me to interview them for the book and the Podcast series: *Your Why Matters Now Everyday Stories* (check this out). While some of you are in this book, others of you will be on the podcast, and others of you gave me great information that helped shape the book. Special thanks to: Jordan Rice, Lydia L. M., Drew Mason, Josh Parker, William Stackler, Maryjane Lueck, Jake Kahut, Stacie Harris, Keyanna Hawkins, David Lyons, Arati Desai Wagabaza, Sowmya Murthy, Caleb Asomugha, Jess Ekstrom, Faraji Muhammad, David Gates, Anthony Gorrity, Katie Eubanks, Kelly Jennings, Dr. Kortni Alston, Jennifer

Eugene, Irene Bailey (big sis), Adam Rees, Nathaniel Benjamin, Tim Hurley, Dr. Tonya Moore, Ralph Clark, Dede Stockton, Mary Hester Clifton, Sherry Lanier, Tiffany Simmons, Scott Southworth, and my amazing mentor who always makes time for me: Forest Harper!

I would like to thank my editor, Darcie Clemen. Your patience and professionalism are amazing. Thank you to my awesome cover designer, Anthony Gorrity, who allowed me to go back and forth many times to get it right. I am thankful for my creative team who worked on the graphics. I am very grateful for Dede Stockton and her team, who helped me organize the interviews and begin much of the research. I would also like to thank you for investing in this book and reading it. I hope that it brings you closer to your Why, Now!

Recommended Reading

While there are countless books and journal articles that will be beneficial on this journey, here are a few that I believe rise above the rest.

p *The 7 Habits of Highly Effective People* by Stephen R. Covey

p *The Now Habit* by Neil Fiore

p *Start with Why* by Simon Sinek

p *Drive* by Daniel Pink

p *The Sleep Revolution* by Arianna Huffington

p *Getting Things Done* by David Allen

p *Nine Things Successful People Do Differently* by Heidi Grant-Halvorson

p *Start* by Jon Acuff

Notes

Chapter 1

1. "'You've Got to Find What You Love,' Jobs says," Stanford News, June 14, 2005, http://news.stanford.edu/2005/06/14/jobs-061505.

Chapter 2

1. Nchorbuno Dominic Abonam, "The Role of Motivation on Employee Performance in The Public Sector: A Case Study of the University for Development Studies–Wa Campus" (master's thesis, Kwame Nkrumah University of Sciences and Technology, 2011), 10, http://ir.knust.edu.gh/bitstream/123456789/4281/1/Dominic%20Abonam%20Nchorbuno.pdf.
2. Daniel Pink, *Drive: The Surprising Truth about What Motivates Us* (New York: Penguin, 2011).

Chapter 3

1. Simon Sinek, "How Great Leaders Inspire Action," Ted.com (TEDxPugetSound talk, 2009), https://www.ted.com/talks/simon_sinek_how_great_leaders_inspire_action.
2. John Bohannon, "One Type of Motivation May Be Key to Success," *Science*, July 1, 2014, http://www.sciencemag.org/news/2014/07/one-type-motivation-may-be-key-success.
3. Anders Dysvik and Bard Kuvaas, "Intrinsic and Extrinsic Motivation as Predictors of Work Effort: The Moderating Role of Achievement Goals," *British Journal of Social Psychology* 52, no.3 (2012): 412–30.

Chapter 5

1. Jessica Amortegui, "Why Finding Meaning at Work Is More Important Than Feeling Happy," *Fast Company*, June 26, 2014, https://www.fastcompany.com/3032126/how-to-find-meaning-during-your-pursuit-of-happiness-at-work.
2. Michael F. Steger, "Meaningful Work," Laboratory for the Study of Meaning and Quality of Life, http://www.michaelfsteger.com/?page_id=105.
3. Jesper Isaksen, "Constructing Meaning Despite the Drudgery of Repetitive Work," *Journal of Humanistic Psychology* 40, no. 3 (2000): 93.
4. Bryan J. Dik and Ryan D. Duffy, "Calling and Vocation at Work," *Counseling Psychologist* 37, no. 3 (2009): 432, http://journals.sagepub.com/doi/abs/10.1177/0011000008316430.
5. Michael F. Steger, Bryan J. Dik, and Ryan D. Duffy, "Measuring Meaningful Work: The Work and Meaning Inventory (WAMI)," *Journal of Career Assessment* 1, no. 16 (2012), http://www.michaelfsteger.com/wp-content/uploads/2012/08/Steger-Dik-Duffy-JCA-in-press.pdf, 2.

6. Teresa Amabile and Steven J. Kramer, "The Power of Small Wins," *Harvard Business Review*, May 2011, https://hbr.org/2011/05/the-power-of-small-wins.

7. Marjolein Lips-Wiersma and Sarah Wright, "Measuring the Meaning of Meaningful Work," *Group & Organization Management*, October 10, 2012, 660.

8. Dik and Duffy, "Calling and Vocation at Work," 430–31.

9. Ibid., 442.

10. Amy Wrzesniewski and Jane E. Dutton, "Crafting a Job," *Academy of Management Review* 26, no. 2 (2001), http://webuser.bus.umich.edu/janedut/POS /craftingajob.pdf, 179.

11. Ibid., 179–80.

12. Ibid., 181.

13. Paul Lyons, "The Crafting of Jobs and Individual Differences" (abstract), *Journal of Business and Psychology* 23, no. 1–2 (2008), https://link.springer.com/article /10.1007/s10869-008-9080-2.

14. Amy Wrzesniewski, et al., "Job Crafting and Cultivating Positive Meaning and Identity in Work," *Advances in Positive Organizational Psychology* 1 (2013), http://justinmberg.com/wrzesniewski-lobuglio-dutto.pdf, 286.

15. Wrzesniewski and Dutton, "Crafting a Job," 180.

16. Dik and Duffy, "Calling and Vocation at Work," 434.

17. Steger, Dik, and Duffy, "Measuring Meaningful Work," 2.

Chapter 6

1. Peter M. Gollwitzer, et al., "When Intentions Go Public: Does Social Reality Widen the Intention-Behavior Gap?" *Psychological Science* 20, no. 5 (2009), http://www.psych.nyu.edu/gollwitzer/09_Gollwitzer_Sheeran_Seifert_Michalski _When_Intentions_.pdf, 612.

2. Heidi Grant Halvorson, *9 Things Successful People Do Differently* (Boston: Harvard Business Review, 2012), 41.

Chapter 7

1. Giovanni B. Moneta and Mihaly Csikszentmihalyi, "The Effect of Perceived Challenges and Skills on the Quality of Subjective Experience," *Journal of Personality* 64, no. 2 (1996): 277, http://onlinelibrary.wiley.com/doi/10.1111/j.1467-6494 .1996.tb00512.x/abstract;jsessionid=FFDA356320BB45B540126F1AB0FBEB9F .f04t03, 277.

2. Steven Kotler, "Create a Work Environment That Fosters Flow," *Harvard Business Review*, May 6, 2014, https://hbr.org/2014/05/create-a-work-environment-that -fosters-flow.

3. Ibid.

4. Wendy Marx, "Careers: Personal Branding and Work-Life Balance," *Fast Company*, November 15, 2007, https://www.fastcompany.com/661205/careers-personal -branding-and-work-life-balance.

5. Sabine Ae Geurts, PhD, and Sabine Sonnentag, PhD, "Recovery as an Explanatory Mechanism in the Relation between Acute Stress Reactions and Chronic Health Impairment," *Scandinavian Journal of Work, Environment & Health* 32, no. 6 (2006), https://kops.uni-konstanz.de/bitstream/handle/123456789/10511

/Recovery_as_an_explanatory_mechanism_in_the_relation_between_acute
_stress_reactions_and_chronic_health_impairment.pdf?sequence=1, 484.

6. Rachel Gillett, "A New Study Shows Saving Your Vacation Time Can Do More Harm Than Good," *Business Insider*, July 15, 2015, http://www.businessinsider.com/consequence-of-not-taking-vacation-2015-7.

7. Charlotte Fritz, Chak Fu Lam, and Gretchen M. Spreitzer, "It's the Little Things That Matter," the Academy of Management Perspectives, August 1, 2011, http://positiveorgs.bus.umich.edu/wp-content/uploads/ItsTheLittleThingsThatMatter.pdf, 3.

8. Ibid.

9. Wido Oerlemans and Arnold Bakker, "Burnout and Daily Recovery: A Day Reconstruction Study," *Journal of Occupational Health Psychology* 19, no. 3 (2014), 308–309, http://dx.doi.org/10.1037/a0036904.

10. Arianna Huffington, *The Sleep Revolution: Transforming Your Life, One Night at a Time* (New York: Harmony Books, 2016), 23.

11. Masaya Takahashi, "Prioritizing Sleep for Healthy Work Schedules," *Journal of Physiological Anthropology* 31, no. 6 (2012), 1. https://jphysiolanthropol.biomedcentral.com/track/pdf/10.1186/1880-6805-31-6?site=jphysiolanthropol.biomedcentral.com.

12. Jitendra M. Mishra, "A Case for Naps in the Workplace," *Seidman Business Review* 15, no. 1 (2009), http://scholarworks.gvsu.edu/cgi/viewcontent.cgi?article=1057&context=sbr.

13. Ibid.

14. Tony Schwartz, "How to Accomplish More by Doing Less," *Harvard Business Review*, December 13, 2011, https://hbr.org/2011/12/how-to-accomplish-more-by-doin.html.

15. K. Anders Ericsson, Ralf Th. Krampe, and Clemens Tesch-Römer, "The Role of Deliberate Practice in the Acquisition of Expert Performance," *Psychological Review* 100, no. 3 (1993), 382.

Chapter 8

1. Maria Konnikova, "The Hazards of Going on Autopilot," *New Yorker*, September 5, 2014, http://www.newyorker.com/science/maria-konnikova/hazards-automation.

2. "Mindfulness and Mindlessness," Psychology, iresearch.net, accessed August 3, 2017, https://psychology.iresearchnet.com/social-psychology/control/mindfulness-and-mindlessness/.

3. Rachel F. Adler and Raquel Benbunan-Fich, "Self-Interruptions in Discretionary Multitasking," *Computers in Human Behavior* 29, March 5, 2013, https://interruptions.net/literature/Adler-ComputHumBehav13.pdf, 1441.

4. Ibid., 1442.

5. Julia Naftulin, "Here's How Many Times We Touch Our Phones Every Day," *Business Insider*, July 13, 2016, http://www.businessinsider.com/dscout-research-people-touch-cell-phones-2617-times-a-day-2016-7.

6. Terri Griffith, "Help Your Employees Find Flow," *Harvard Business Review*, April 17, 2014, https://hbr.org/2014/04/help-your-employees-find-flow.

7. Cynthia D. Fisher, "Effects of External and Internal Interruptions on Boredom at Work: Two Studies," *Journal of Organizational Behavior* 19, no. 5 (1998), https://interruptions.net/literature/Fisher-JOrganizBehav98.pdf, 505.
8. Adler and Benbunan-Fich, "Self-Interruptions in Discretionary Multitasking," 1443.
9. Carol Dweck, "What Having a Growth Mindset Really Means," *Harvard Business Review*, January 13, 2016, https://hbr.org/2016/01/what-having-a-growth-mindset-actually-means.
10. Tony Schwartz and Catherine McCarthy, "Manage Your Energy, Not Your Time," *Harvard Business Review*, October 2007, https://hbr.org/2007/10/manage-your-energy-not-your-time.

Chapter 9

1. Teresa Amabile and Steven J. Kramer, "The Power of Small Wins," *Harvard Business Review*, May 2011, https://hbr.org/2011/05/the-power-of-small-wins.
2. Martin E. P. Seligman, "Building Resilience," *Harvard Business Review*, April 2011, https://hbr.org/2011/04/building-resilience.

Chapter 10

1. Neil Fiore, *The Now Habit: A Strategic Program for Overcoming Procrastination* (New York: Penguin, 2007), 25.
2. Scott Spreier, Mary H. Fontaine, and Ruth Malloy, "Leadership Run Amok: The Destructive Potential of Overachievers," *Harvard Business Review*, June 2006, https://hbr.org/2006/06/leadership-run-amok-the-destructive-potential-of-overachievers.

Chapter 11

1. W. D. Hamilton, "Geometry for the Selfish Herd," *Journal of Theoretical Biology* 31, no. 2 (1971): 295–311, http://www.csun.edu/~dgray/BE528/Hamilton1971 Selfish_herd.pdf.
2. "Motivation in Today's Workplace: The Link to Performance," *Society for Human Resource Management Research Quarterly*, 2010, https://www.shrm.org/Resources AndTools/tools-and-samples/toolkits/Documents/10-0235%20Research%20 Quarterly-Q2-FNL.pdf.
3. "Prosci Change Management Methodology Overview," Prosci.com, https://www.prosci.com/change-management/thought-leadership-library/change-management-methodology-overview.

Chapter 12

1. Christopher Michaelson, et al., "Meaningful Work: Connecting Business Ethics and Organization Studies," *Journal of Business Ethics* 121, no. 1 (2014): 80–81, https://www.researchgate.net/publication/257542225_Meaningful_Work_Connecting_Business_Ethics_and_Organization_Studies.
2. Yu-Hsuan Wang, et al., "Antecedents and Outcomes of Career Plateaus: The Roles of Mentoring Others and Proactive Personality," *Journal of Vocational Behavior* 85, no. 3 (2014): 319, http://www.sciencedirect.com/science/article/pii/S0001879114001043.